Handbook California Design

30–1965
aftspeople, Designers,
anufacturers

Edited by
Bobbye Tigerman

With contributions by
Jennifer Munro Miller
Lacy Simkowitz
Staci Steinberger
Bobbye Tigerman

Los Angeles County Museum of Art

The MIT Press
Cambridge, Massachusetts
London, England

This book is a companion to the catalogue for *California Design, 1930–1965: "Living in a Modern Way,"* an exhibition on view at the Los Angeles County Museum of Art from October 1, 2011, through June 3, 2012.

This publication was made possible in part by the Andrew W. Mellon Foundation and the Craft Research Fund of the Center for Craft, Creativity & Design, a Center of UNC Asheville.

Copublished by the Los Angeles County Museum of Art, 5905 Wilshire Boulevard, Los Angeles, CA, 90036, and the MIT Press, 55 Hayward Street, Cambridge, MA, 02142

MIT Press books may be purchased at special quantity discounts for business or sales promotional use. For information, please email special_sales@mitpress.mit .edu or write to Special Sales Department, The MIT Press, 55 Hayward Street, Cambridge, MA, 02142

Complete illustration credits are found on pp. 310–11. Most photographs are reproduced courtesy of the creators and lenders of the material depicted. For certain artwork and documentary photographs, we have been unable to trace copyright holders. The publishers would appreciate notification of additional credits for acknowledgment in future editions.

Library of Congress Cataloging-in-Publication Data

A handbook of California design, 1930–1965 : craftspeople, designers, manufacturers / edited by Bobbye Tigerman ; with contributions by Jennifer Munro Miller, Lacy Simkowitz, Staci Steinberger, and Bobbye Tigerman.
    p.   cm
This book is a companion to the catalogue for California Design, 1930–1965: Living in a Modern Way, an exhibition on view at the Los Angeles County Museum of Art from October 1, 2011, through June 3, 2012.
Includes bibliographical references.
ISBN 978-0-262-51838-3 (pbk. : alk. paper)
1. Decorative arts—California—History—20th century. 2. Modernism (Aesthetics)—California. 3. Artisans—California—Biography. 4. Designers—California—Biography. I. Title: California design, 1930–1965.
NK835.C3C35   2011 Suppl.
745.09794'0904—dc23
                    2012031528

LACMA Head of Publications: Lisa Gabrielle Mark
Project Manager: Nola Butler
Content Editor: Wendy Kaplan
Editor: Dianne Woo
Production: The Production Department
Publications Administrator: Monica Paniry
Supervising Photographer: Peter Brenner
Photo Editor: Staci Steinberger
Rights and Reproductions: Piper Severance, Jeanne Dreskin, and Maia November
Proofreader: Richard G. Gallin

This book was designed by Irma Boom. It was first published in an edition of 5,000 copies in 2013. Composed in Neuzeit and Replica on 100 gsm Yulong woodfree, it was printed and bound in China.

Page 1: John Follis and James Reed, *Arts and Architecture* (magazine cover), September 1953. Collection of Los Angeles Modern Auctions (LAMA). Reprinted courtesy David Travers.

Pages 2–3, 4–5, 314–15, 316–17, 318–19: Exhibition installation shots of *California Design, 1930–1965: "Living in a Modern Way"* at the Los Angeles County Museum of Art, Los Angeles, California.

Page 312: Deborah Sussman, *Six More* (exhibition catalogue), 1963. The Mr. and Mrs. Allan C. Balch Research Library, Los Angeles County Museum of Art.

Page 320: Sam Hyde Harris for Southern Pacific Company, *Southern Pacific's New Daylight* (poster), c. 1937. LACMA, Gift of Debbie and Mark Attanasio in memory of Martin Kaplan. Courtesy of Union Pacific Railroad.

Contents

It gives me great pleasure to present this handbook of California craftspeople, designers, and manufacturers, a testament to the Los Angeles County Museum of Art's abiding commitment to California design. It is a companion volume to the catalogue for the landmark exhibition *California Design, 1930–1965: "Living in a Modern Way,"* which was on view at LACMA from fall 2011 to spring 2012. As a complement to that major scholarly achievement, this work consists of more than 140 biographies documenting the most influential craft and design practitioners active in California between 1930 and 1965. The first book to provide biographical information and new research about many of its subjects, it will serve as an invaluable reference for scholars, students, collectors, and all those interested in California design.

This book reflects LACMA's dedication to the study and preservation of California design. By publishing new scholarship, organizing public programs, and collecting key works, LACMA strives to be a central repository of information for specialists and the public alike. The museum's California design collection, which has expanded by over one hundred objects since the initiative began in 2006, continues to grow and represent the wide range of design innovation that occurred in California.

For more than five years, Wendy Kaplan, Decorative Arts and Design department head and curator, and Bobbye Tigerman, Decorative Arts and Design associate curator, have devoted their formidable intelligence, passion, and diligence to creating a lasting legacy for California design at LACMA. Through their ground-breaking exhibition and catalogue, and by establishing a significant collection of objects for the museum, they have allowed future generations to appreciate how the ideal of "modern living" developed in California in the mid-twentieth century. This book represents their continuing quest to document the state's design contributions; it emerged from the realization that years of research could not be contained in a single exhibition catalogue. There just was too much important information about these great designers—and their designs too great—not to publish their biographies for future study.

I am deeply grateful to those who made this book possible, especially to Will Ferrell and Viveca Paulin-Ferrell and Peter and Shannon Loughrey for their early, generous support. I also thank LACMA's Decorative Arts and Design Council; the Center for Craft, Creativity & Design; and the Elsie de Wolfe Foundation for their vital contributions. Their support of this initiative allows LACMA to fulfill its mission of collecting extraordinary works of art and interpreting them for a broad audience.

Michael Govan
CEO and Wallis Annenberg Director
Los Angeles County Museum of Art

Bobbye Tigerman

Addressing his fellow California architects, designers, and manufacturers in 1947, the eminent designer Alvin Lustig observed, "It is common practice today to place the word 'California' in front of almost any vagrant word and thus achieve a magic combination hopefully intended to make the heart jump and the purse strings fly open."[1] Lustig was likely referring to the widespread perception among both California's denizens and the rest of the country that the Golden State was a place characterized by unlimited opportunity, a romantic, carefree attitude, and freedom from the shackles of tradition. Always regarded as an earthly paradise where barriers to entry were low and the future was not just imagined but already being lived, California was a breeding ground for new ideas to flourish without constraint. It was a center for technical and material innovation, where prewar and World War II developments in the defense and aerospace industries found consumer applications. At the same time, the abundance of institutions of higher learning yielded a large, well-educated class of designers and craftspeople.

The Art Center School (home to the first industrial design program in Southern California) was especially committed to providing a high-quality, practical art education: its mission, as stated in a 1931 brochure, was "to produce, in the most limited time practical, artists who are able to successfully enter the business world and immediately reap the rewards of careful training."[2] Many other institutions were established throughout the state as part of the public education system built after World War II. These training grounds provided jobs for educators and opportunities for students to work in creative fields, many of whom matriculated through the GI Bill, which allowed World War II veterans to pursue higher education and vocational training. All of these factors converged to create a fertile environment for the design and production of consumer goods that stimulated the postwar economy and helped to define the enviably high American standard of living at mid-century. While a more recent generation of scholars has asserted that these ideas about freedom, boundless opportunity, and unfailingly clement weather were part myth, the notion of California as a land of opportunity attracted throngs to the Golden State over its long history, fueling its economy and creative output. The personal and professional narratives of the craftspeople, designers, and manufacturers featured in this book collectively illustrate how these perceptions—and often clichés—about California's promise shaped the material lives of a nation.

This handbook is the product of research conducted for the exhibition *California Design, 1930–1965: "Living in a Modern Way,"* which was on view at the Los Angeles County Museum of Art from October 1, 2011, to June 3, 2012. Curated by Wendy Kaplan and myself, it was the first exhibition to explore how California design shaped American material culture before and after World War II, examining the roots of modernism in the state, the contributions of émigré designers, the postwar transition to a Cold War economy, and the marketing and dissemination

(From left) Hansel Mieth, Frans Wildenhain, Marguerite Wildenhain, Victor Ries, and Trude Guermonprez at Pond Farm Workshops, c. 1949.

of California design throughout the country and the world. It brought together a full range of design media, including furniture, fashion, textiles, jewelry, ceramics, graphic and industrial design, and period film footage. With major support from the Getty Foundation through the Pacific Standard Time initiative, we conducted extensive research and unearthed much previously unknown information. The research team visited libraries, archives, and private collections; interviewed designers and their descendants; and thoroughly examined period books and magazines. The succinct biographies found here serve as an introductory resource for all those interested in California design. For those whose work is well documented, their biographies synthesize a large literature. For those who have not been extensively studied, their entries make this information widely available for the first time.

Following the parameters of the exhibition, this handbook includes designers, craftspeople, and manufacturers who were active between 1930 and 1965. California experienced a perpetual population boom from the beginning of the twentieth century, and 1930 marks the point when an influx of newcomers arrived as a result of the Great Depression, the growth of the oil industry and the

Hollywood film industry, and the general perception of opportunity and a higher quality of life compared to those in other regions of the country. Continuing through the paradigm-shifting years of World War II, this volume profiles artisans who established independent design careers before 1965, when dramatic transformations altered the values and modes of production in the design and craft fields. The increasing availability of low-cost imported goods diminished the market for higher-priced domestically made wares. At the same time, the ideal of the designer-craftsman, who produced well-made goods and was self-supported by his or her work, was rapidly being supplanted by the artist-craftsman, who considered the work an avenue of self-expression and increasingly used fine art methods of representation and distribution to reach the public.

The biographies have been carefully selected to represent significant figures from the period 1930 to 1965 and the full range of design disciplines. While the scope of this publication is limited to designers, craftspeople, and manufacturers included in the exhibition, there were some individuals for whom we could not find a suitable object to show, yet they played such an important role that they merited inclusion in this book. Both native Californians and transplants who established their careers in the state are included. Some, such as Harry Bertoia, Henry Dreyfuss, and Claire Falkenstein, worked in California for only a portion of their careers and had significant periods of productivity elsewhere. The entries for these individuals focus on their achievements during their California period. Although some of the subjects were architects as well as designers, this book does not include those whose work was predominantly architecture or landscape architecture owing to an already vast literature on those subjects and many dedicated monographs. Some figures were not included because of extensive information available in other sources, especially those published in conjunction with the Pacific Standard Time initiative.

No less a figure than Charles Eames declared, "the connections, the connections. It will in the end be these details that provide service to the customer and give the product its life."[3] Referring to mechanical connections, he could also have been talking about the importance of collaboration and cooperation vital to all creative endeavors. Like many design communities of this era, California designers and craftspeople were highly connected. A gathering called the Design Group, which counted among its members many acolytes of Alvin Lustig, including Louis Danziger, Frederick A. Usher Jr., John Follis, Rex Goode, and Charles Kratka, met regularly in Los Angeles in the early 1950s. Working in fields that ranged from graphic to exhibition to environmental to product design, these individuals came together to share their work and discuss design trends, and often collaborated on projects. Further, groups such as the Metal Arts Guild in San Francisco, a regular gathering of metalworkers and jewelers; the Allied Craftsmen in San Diego, an assembly of various craftspeople that convened frequently and exhibited together; and the Architectural Panel, a Los Angeles–based group that organized exhibitions and a highly acclaimed speaker series on architectural issues, established connections that bound the design community together.

Connections did not have to be highly institutionalized, either. Harrison McIntosh and Rupert Deese worked in a ceramic studio adjacent to McIntosh's Padua Hills home, where they shared equipment and glazes. In San Francisco, industrial designer Gene Tepper, surface designer Don Smith, landscape designer Lawrence Halprin, and architecture firms Marquis & Stoller and Campbell & Wong shared office space at 802 Montgomery Street, where they ran independent practices but collaborated when opportunities arose. This complicated web sustained design innovation and fueled collaborative practice. Revealing these links, and the crucial connective role played by art and design schools, museums, and other arts institutions, is a key objective of this book and is demonstrated visually in the infographic on pages 16–17. In addition, whenever a subject is mentioned in another's biography, the name appears in orange boldface, directing the reader to the related entry. To further assist the reader, a list of frequently used acronyms is found on page 19.

A Handbook of California Design, 1930–1965: Craftspeople, Designers, Manufacturers serves as an introduction to this vast subject and offers guidance for further research. As such, each entry ends with a list of specific sources. A list of further reading at the back of the book directs the interested researcher to additional and more general resources on the subject. In his seminal article on modern California design, Alvin Lustig proclaimed that "something flies into your mind when the magic phrase 'California Modern' is uttered."[4] I hope that this book sparks the same magic for future generations of California design students and scholars.

1.
Alvin Lustig, "California Modern," *Designs* (Hollywood, Calif.), October 1947, 8.
2.
104 Years of Experience (Pasadena: Art Center School, 1931), brochure.
3.
ECS, directed by Charles and Ray Eames (Zeeland, Mich.: Herman Miller Furniture Company, 1961), film.
4.
Lustig, "California Modern," 8.

Connections and Collaborations

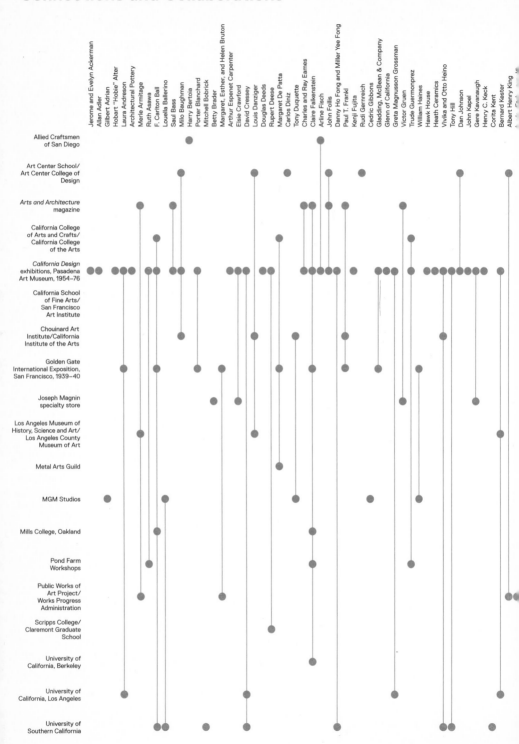

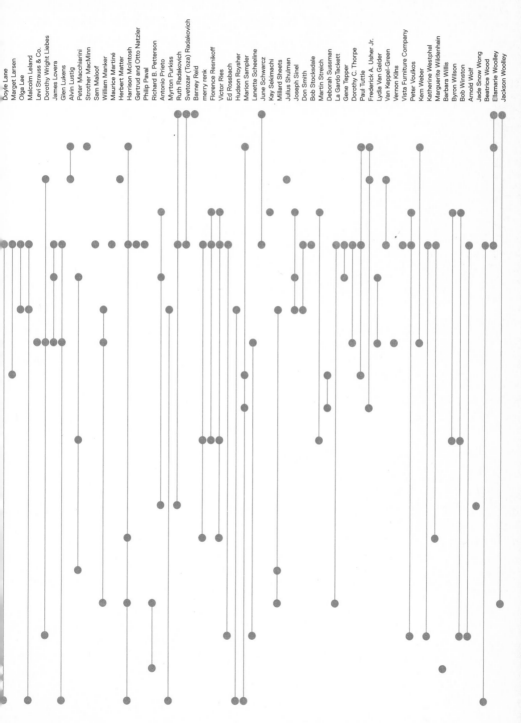

Doyle Lane
Marget Larsen
Olga Lee
Malcolm Leland
Levi Strauss & Co.
Dorothy Wright Liebes
James Lovera
Glen Lukens
Alvin Lustig
Peter Macchiarini
Strother MacMinn
Sam Maloof
William Manker
Maurice Martiné
Herbert Matter
Harrison McIntosh
Gertrud and Otto Natzler
Philip Paval
Richard B. Petterson
Antonio Prieto
Myrton Purkiss
Ruth Radakovich
Svetozar (Toza) Radakovich
Barney Reid
merry renk
Florence Resnikoff
Victor Ries
Ed Rossbach
Hudson Roysher
Marion Sampler
Lanette Scheeline
June Schwarcz
Kay Sekimachi
Millard Sheets
Julius Shulman
Joseph Sinel
Don Smith
Bob Stocksdale
Martin Streich
Deborah Sussman
La Gardo Tackett
Gene Tepper
Dorothy C. Thorpe
Paul Tuttle
Frederick A. Usher Jr.
Lydia Van Gelder
Van Keppel–Green
Vernon Kilns
Vista Furniture Company
Peter Voulkos
Kem Weber
Katherine Westphal
Marguerite Wildenhain
Barbara Willis
Byron Wilson
Bob Winston
Arnold Wolf
Jade Snow Wong
Beatrice Wood
Ellamarie Woolley
Jackson Woolley

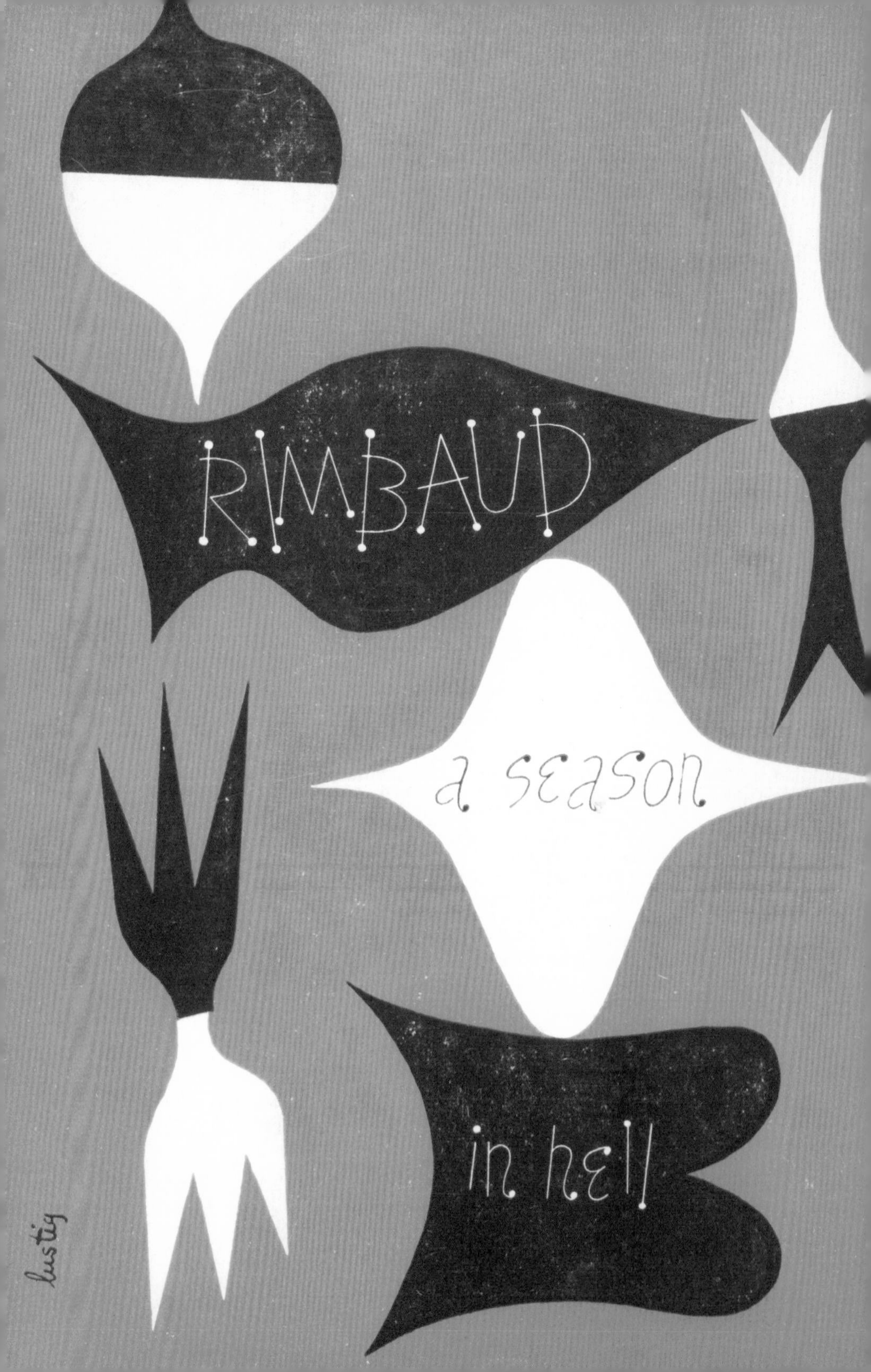
RIMBAUD
a season
in hell
lustig

The authors of the biographical entries are
identified by their initials as follows:

Jennifer Munro Miller	JMM
Lacy Simkowitz	LS
Staci Steinberger	SS
Bobbye Tigerman	BT

Frequently Used Acronyms

AIGA	American Institute of Graphic Arts
CCAC	California College of Arts and Crafts
LACMA	Los Angeles County Museum of Art
MGM	Metro-Goldwyn-Mayer Studios
MoMA	Museum of Modern Art, New York
SFMOMA	San Francisco Museum of Modern Art
UCLA	University of California, Los Angeles
USC	University of Southern California

Alvin Lustig for New Directions Publishing, *A Season in Hell* (book cover), 1945.
Museum of California Design, Gift of Mark and Maura Resnick.

Evelyn Ackerman
b. 1924
Jerome Ackerman
b. 1920

Evelyn and Jerome Ackerman successfully combined craft and design in their work, creating an array of affordable products for residential and architectural use that included ceramics, mosaics, wall hangings, carved wood panels, and cabinet hardware. Married in 1948, the couple grew up only blocks apart in Detroit. Evelyn earned a BFA (1945) and an MFA (1950) at Wayne State University. After completing an undergraduate degree at the same institution, Jerome received an MFA from the prestigious ceramics program at Alfred University in New York (1952). Attracted by the temperate climate and promise of opportunity, they relocated to Los Angeles in 1952 and established Jenev Design Studio that year. (The name was a combination of the letters in *Jerome* and *Evelyn*.) The Ackermans began producing slip-cast ceramics and added mosaics to their repertoire in 1955. They formed ERA Industries in 1956 and opened their first showroom in 1959. The artists designed and created products in diverse media and styles ranging from the sleek, modern forms of their early ceramics to colorful, stylized figural designs inspired by folk art. As the business expanded, their designs were produced in small workshops in the United States, Japan, and Mexico. The couple combined a willingness to experiment with new production methods and materials with a knowledge of and appreciation for traditional craft skills. By the late 1980s they had closed their showroom and were focusing on individual projects. Their work was included in every *California Design* show and was the subject of an exhibition at Mingei International Museum in San Diego (2009). JMM

Sources
· Joyce Lovelace, "Masters of Mid-Century California Modernism," *American Craft*, June/July 2009, 32–39.
· Jeffrey Head, "Design Duo: Jerome and Evelyn Ackerman," *Modernism* 8, no. 1 (Spring 2005): 76–83.
· Ackerman: The Mid-Century Modern Works of Jerome & Evelyn Ackerman (website), www.ackermanmodern.com.
· Study files, Balch Art Research Library, LACMA, DEC.002.

Silversmith Allan Adler was renowned for the functional simplicity of his designs and for fashioning a vast array of flatware, hollowware, and jewelry, often devising his own tools and adapting new machines and technologies to bring more efficient methods to a traditional, handwrought craft. Originally from Missoula, Montana, Adler moved with his family to Southern California as an infant. Not formally educated in crafts, he began apprenticing with his father-in-law, silversmith Porter Blanchard, soon after he married Porter's daughter Rebecca in 1938. In 1940, when Blanchard moved his operation to Pacoima in the San Fernando Valley, Adler took over Blanchard's Sunset Boulevard shop in Los Angeles, where, as Allan Adler, Inc., he and his team of craftspeople created silver objects in the workshop below the retail store. Despite limited materials, Adler kept his nascent business going during World War II with a government contract to produce silver tubes essential for use in radar. After the war, Adler's designs, often inspired by early American, Scandinavian, and Chinese sources, became popular with the Hollywood elite, enabling him to open shops in Corona del Mar and La Jolla (in Southern California) and in San Francisco, where in the 1960s he owned and operated the V. C. Morris gift shop designed by Frank Lloyd Wright (1948–49). Adler silver was also sold in exclusive specialty stores nationwide. When a fire destroyed the Sunset Boulevard workshop in 1980, he built a new facility in the San Fernando Valley. Adler was the recipient of numerous high-profile commissions, including crowns for the Miss Universe and Miss USA pageants (1953), and his work appeared in both national and international exhibitions such as *Good Design* at MoMA and *Design for Use, USA* (1951–53). JMM

Sources
· Mary Rourke, "Allan Adler, 86; Crafted Beauty Queens' Crowns, Silver Pieces for the Stars," *Los Angeles Times*, December 5, 2002.
· Robert Sommers, "Allan Adler: Modern Silver Master, Part Two." *Silver Magazine* 31, no. 1 (January/February 1999): 24–29.
· Robert Sommers, "Allan Adler: Modern Silver Master, Part One," *Silver Magazine* 30, no. 6 (November/December 1998): 32–42.
· Janice Lovoos, "Two California Silversmiths: Roysher and Adler," *American Artist* 21, no. 3 (March 1957): 50–55, 61–62.

Born Adrian Greenburg in Naugatuck, Connecticut, the famed Hollywood costume designer and couturier known as Adrian created high-style fashion that combined glamour, versatility, and practicality. Adrian attended the New York School of Fine and Applied Art, but, after transferring to the school's Paris branch in 1922, he returned to New York to design for Irving Berlin's *Music Box Revue*. In 1925 he moved to Los Angeles to work on a Rudolph Valentino film and began designing costumes for the Cecil B. DeMille studios the following year. Adrian followed DeMille to MGM, where he designed for more than two hundred films, including *Marie Antoinette*, *The Wizard of Oz*, and *The Philadelphia Story*. Adrian became a household name as Hollywood costume design became an indispensable part of popular culture, and his creations were seen by millions in movie theaters and in the press. He is often credited as the originator of the modern, broad-shouldered silhouette predominant from the mid-1930s through the 1940s. When war broke out in Europe and imports of French couture became scarce, Adrian capitalized on the opportunity to start his own fashion business. He left MGM in 1941 and launched Adrian Ltd. in 1942 in Beverly Hills, specializing in both couture and ready-to-wear clothing. His innovative yet wearable collections featured vibrant color combinations, asymmetrical draping, whimsical and exotic prints, and V-shaped silhouettes. After suffering a heart attack in 1952, he closed the business and spent several years recuperating in Brazil with his wife, actress Janet Gaynor, and their son. They moved back to L.A. in 1957, and he resumed work. Adrian was designing costumes for a stage production of *Camelot* at the time of his death. JMM

Sources
· Christian Esquevin, *Adrian: Silver Screen to Custom Label* (New York: Monacelli Press, 2008).
· Howard Gutner, *Gowns by Adrian: The MGM Years, 1928–1941* (New York: Abrams, 2001).
· Virginia Scallon, "The Adrian Story," *The Californian*, May 1950, 20–21, 62.

A proselytizer for the pleasure and freedom of road travel, Wallace "Wally" Byam (1896–1962), founder of Airstream Trailer Company, touted his products as the key to living a comfortable mobile life. Byam began building custom trailers as a hobby while working in advertising for the *Los Angeles Times*. He introduced the name Airstream in 1934 in classified advertisements he placed in *Popular Mechanics*. The following year Byam purchased the bankrupt trailer company Bowlus-Teller, giving him access to aviator William Hawley Bowlus's design for a streamlined trailer with a riveted aluminum shell derived from airplanes. He modified Bowlus's *Road Chief* with luxury features and reintroduced it in 1936 as the Airstream *Clipper*, a reference to the Pan Am *Clipper* airplane, which it resembled. In addition to this expensive model, the company offered more affordable wood and Masonite options. When World War II restrictions on aluminum forced Airstream to drastically cut production, Byam found supplemental work at the Curtiss-Wright aircraft factory, where he learned about advanced power tools and construction techniques. In 1948 he relaunched Airstream with a factory in Van Nuys, hiring skilled craftsmen from the aircraft industry. Airstream trailers gained a devoted following, and beginning in 1955, Byam organized the Wally Byam International Caravan Club, leading enthusiasts on widely publicized road trips around the world. The company added a factory in Jackson Center, Ohio, in 1952, which became the primary headquarters after the Van Nuys plant closed in 1979. Now owned by Thor Industries, the company continues to produce modified versions of the original designs. ss

Sources
- *Airstream Life*, Green Cove Springs, Fla.: Church Street Publishing, 2004–present.
- Russ Banham, *Wanderlust: Airstream at 75* (Old Saybrook, Conn.: Greenwich Publishing Group, 2005).
- Bryan Burkhart and David Hunt, *Airstream: The History of the Land Yacht* (San Francisco: Chronicle Books, 2000).
- Wally Byam, *Trailer Travel Here and Abroad: The New Way to Adventurous Living* (New York: David McKay, 1961).

Wallace "Wally" Byam, founder of Airstream Trailer Company.

Hobart "Hobie" Alter
b. 1933

Native Californian Hobart "Hobie" Alter was a pioneer in the development of foam and fiberglass surfboards, recreational water equipment, and catamaran design. Born in Upland and raised in Ontario, Alter began shaping balsa-wood surfboards in the garage of his family's Laguna Beach summer home while still in high school. He attended Chaffey Junior College and fabricated surfboards in the summer before opening Hobie Surf Shop in Dana Point in 1954. With Gordon "Grubby" Clark, who worked for him as a glasser (one who lays fiberglass), Alter developed a marketable polyurethane foam surfboard blank in 1958. The pair soon established a foam-blowing operation in Laguna Canyon, which Clark took over in 1961. (Clark Foam went on to become the largest surfboard blank manufacturer until closing abruptly in 2005.) Alter capitalized on the explosion of surf culture in the late 1950s and 1960s with his lightweight, easily shaped boards and created a brand name that became synonymous with surfing and watersports. He continued to experiment with innovative materials and expanded his product line to include skateboards, sportswear, and the *Hobie Cat*, a best-selling catamaran. JMM

Sources
· Drew Kampion, *Greg Noll: The Art of the Surfboard* (Layton, Utah: Gibbs Smith, 2007).
· Mark Blackburn, *Surf's Up: Collecting the Longboard Era* (Atglen, Pa.: Schiffer, 2001).
· Andrew Rusnak, "Fun in the Son," part 2, *Composites Fabrication*, June 2001, 2–9.
· Andrew Rusnak, "Fun in the Son," part 1, *Composites Fabrication*, May 2001, 2–10.
· Bob Duke, "Hobie's Power Trip," *Motor Boating & Sailing*, May 1998, 60–63, 118.

Laura Andreson
1902–1999

A leading figure among vessel potters, Laura Andreson experimented widely with clay bodies and glaze types and taught ceramics to hundreds of students, beginning at a time when few schools offered instruction in the medium. A lifelong resident of Los Angeles, she earned a BA from UCLA (1932), where she studied with Olive Newcomb, and an MA in painting from Columbia University (1936). As a professor in the art department at UCLA from 1933 to 1970, Andreson learned ceramic techniques through trial and error and by seeking advice from other ceramists. In 1944 Gertrud Natzler taught her how to throw clay on a wheel, and she learned similar practices from students whom she had sent to study with F. Carlton Ball at Mills College. Andreson initially worked in earthenware, producing hand-built or slip-cast forms with tooled and incised surface decoration. She later worked in stoneware and after 1957 turned to porcelain as her primary medium. Proficient at both throwing and glaze chemistry, she received several grants to research and develop original glaze formulas. Summing up her work in 1985, Andreson declared, "My forms are inspired by the perfection of the egg form and the thinness of its shell, and from forms found in nature rather than from manmade objects."[1] BT

1.
Crocker Art Museum, *The Creative Arts League Presents California Crafts XIV* (Sacramento: The League, 1985), 64.

Sources
- Laura Andreson Papers, 1902–1991, Archives of American Art, Smithsonian Institution.
- *Laura Andreson: A Retrospective in Clay*, exh. cat. (La Jolla, Calif.: Mingei International Museum, 1982).

31

Architectural Pottery
1950–1985

Ubiquitous accessories for the patio or living room, Architectural Pottery's line of ceramics embodied the ideal of versatile design for indoor/outdoor living and became an icon of modern California style. In 1949 La Gardo Tackett challenged his graduate students at the California School of Art in Los Angeles to update planter designs using molds for traditional terracotta pots. The class set to work developing geometric and biomorphic pots and stands that elevated the plants so that the containers could be used both indoors and out. Two of Tackett's students, John Follis and Rex Goode, struggled to produce these designs commercially until 1950, when they founded Architectural Pottery with business manager Rita Lawrence and her husband, Max. After gaining early recognition in trade magazines and exhibitions—notably MoMA's *Good Design* (1950)—the firm developed a following among architects and designers who specified the planters for their commissions. In subsequent years the company added forms by Paul McCobb, Malcolm Leland, and Raul A. Coronel, among others. Production was initially subcontracted, but in the early 1960s the company began to manufacture its own products using a range of techniques, including molding, casting, and jiggering. Demand for larger, lighter planters led to the launch of the Architectural Fiberglass division in 1961, which employed the talents of Follis, Douglas Deeds, and Elsie Crawford in the design of large-scale planters, outdoor seating, and trash receptacles. In 1966 the company added the Pro/Artisan Collection, formalizing an earlier program of hand-finished stoneware by David Cressey. All of the divisions were combined under parent company Group Artec in 1971. By this time the firm had more than two hundred employees, with factories in Oxnard, Maywood, and Manhattan Beach. Architectural Pottery closed in 1985 following a devastating fire. ss

Sources
- Max and Rita Lawrence, Architectural Pottery Records (Collection 1587), Department of Special Collections, Charles E. Young Research Library, University of California, Los Angeles.
- Max and Rita Lawrence, "A Better World through Good Design," interview by Teresa Barnett, 2000, Oral History Program, University of California, Los Angeles.
- Dan MacMasters, "A Gentle Kind of Genius," *Los Angeles Times*, February 13, 1972.

ARCHITECTURAL POTTERY

2020 SOUTH ROBERTSON BOULEVARD • LOS ANGELES 34, CALIFORNIA • UPTON 0-9737

PLANTERS / SAND URNS / SCULPTURE / SPACE DIVIDERS

Architectural Pottery company catalogue, March 1961.

Merle Armitage
1893–1975

A true impresario, Merle Armitage had a long career as an author, designer, and champion of modern expression in all forms. The Iowa native moved to Los Angeles in 1923 and drew on his experience as a concert promoter to found and manage the Los Angeles Grand Opera Association. Armitage became an influential figure in the city's small avant-garde community and a core member of the circle that gathered at Jake Zeitlin's influential bookstore. He promoted and collected the work of local artists, including Elise Cavanna (his wife from 1934 until the early 1940s), Paul Landacre, Millard Sheets, and Henrietta Shore, as well as European modernists. During 1933 and 1934 Armitage was regional director of the Public Works of Art Project, a precursor to the Works Progress Administration. Convinced that contemporary American art scholarship was lacking, he initiated a series of monographs in 1932 on avant-garde artists and performers such as Edward Weston, Igor Stravinsky, and Martha Graham. Armitage designed concert publicity and theater sets prior to moving west, but with this series he embarked on a new career as a book designer. He rejected hidebound rules of the field, instead arguing (in numerous essays as well as in his layouts) that a book's format should echo its content. His books garnered attention for their bold title spreads, which served as poster-like introductions to spacious arrangements of text. Armitage wrote and designed more than eighty books, many related to his numerous passions, which ranged from railroads to gourmet cooking. *Fit for a King: The Merle Armitage Book of Food* (1939) featured recipes from celebrated contributors such as Rockwell Kent, Raymond Loewy, and Lewis Mumford. In 1947 he became art director of *Look* magazine in New York and served as president of the AIGA in the early 1950s before returning to Southern California in 1954. ss

Sources
· Merle Armitage Collection, Press Coll. Archives Armitage, William Andrews Clark Memorial Library, University of California, Los Angeles.
· Merle Armitage Papers, 1932–1964, Special Collections Department, University of Iowa Library, Iowa City. Donated by Merle Armitage.
· Victoria Dailey, Michael Dawson, and Natalie Shivers, *LA's Early Moderns* (Glendale: Balcony Press, 2003), 17–115.
· Merle Armitage, *Merle Armitage's Accent on Life* (Ames: Iowa State University Press, 1965).   .

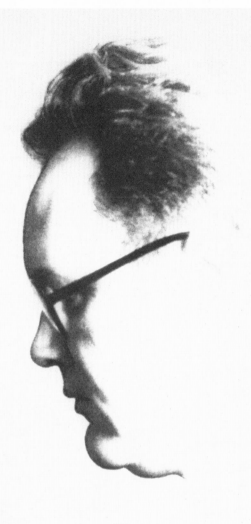

"Merle Armitage"   Will Connell '4.

Born in Norwalk, the daughter of Japanese immigrants, Ruth Asawa skillfully manipulated metal wire into delicate yet powerful sculptural constructions. Following the attack on Pearl Harbor in 1941, Asawa and her family were interned first at Santa Anita racetrack, where she took art classes with Disney animator and fellow internee Tom Okamoto, and later at Rohwer Relocation Center in Arkansas. In 1943 she was allowed to enroll at Milwaukee State Teachers College with plans to become an art teacher. Asawa subsequently attended Black Mountain College in North Carolina (1946–49), where she studied drawing, design, and color theory with Bauhaus émigré Josef Albers and also met her future husband, architect Albert Lanier. Initially focusing on drawing and painting, she later began experimenting with three-dimensional wire sculpture using a looping technique that she learned in Mexico in 1948. Asawa moved to San Francisco in 1949 and became well known for her looped-wire and, later, tied-wire sculptures. In 1965 she accepted a fellowship at the Tamarind Lithography Workshop in Los Angeles, which allowed her to develop a body of printmaking work related to her earlier drawings. She maintained strong alliances with many San Francisco craftspeople, and her intricate pieces appeared in *Four Artists* (1954), an exhibition at the San Francisco Museum of Art (now SFMOMA), which also included work by weaver Ida Dean, jeweler merry renk, and ceramist Marguerite Wildenhain. She received monographic shows at the Pasadena Art Museum (1965), the San Francisco Museum of Art (1973), and the M. H. de Young Museum (2006), among other venues. In the late 1960s Asawa became involved in several civic art initiatives: she cofounded the Alvarado Art Workshop at the elementary school her children attended, and she served on the San Francisco Arts Commission and the California Arts Council. BT

Sources
· Daniell Cornell, *The Sculpture of Ruth Asawa: Contours in the Air*, exh. cat. (San Francisco and Berkeley: Fine Arts Museums of San Francisco and University of California Press, 2006).
· Ruth Asawa and Albert Lanier, interview by Mark Johnson and Paul Karlstrom, June 21–July 5, 2002, Archives of American Art, Smithsonian Institution.
· Gerald Nordland, *Ruth Asawa: A Retrospective View*, exh. cat. (San Francisco: San Francisco Museum of Art, 1973).

F. Carlton Ball
1911–1992

F. Carlton Ball was a widely influential potter and art professor known for his monumental ceramic works, his experimentation and innovation with a range of clay bodies and glazes, and his development of ceramic equipment. His work ran the gamut from earthy stoneware vessels to human-scale textured and decorated vases to playable ceramic musical instruments. Originally from Sutter Creek, near Sacramento, Ball earned degrees in fine arts at USC (BA, 1934; MA, 1935), where ceramics and jewelry classes with Glen Lukens introduced the young artist to the crafts and launched his career as a potter and educator. He taught ceramics and other art subjects at CCAC, Mills College, and USC and at several institutions in the Midwest and Washington State. A dedicated educator and tireless promoter of ceramics, Ball demonstrated wheel throwing at the Golden Gate International Exposition's Art in Action booth in 1940. The Mills College Ceramic Guild—established by Ball and Elena Netherby—allowed members access to the ceramic studio in exchange for dues, which in turn financed equipment and supplies for the college. He also exhibited his work frequently in the *California Design* exhibitions, the *Ceramic National Exhibitions* at the Syracuse Museum of Fine Arts, and countless other shows. Ball extended his influence by writing a regular column on ceramics technique in *Ceramics Monthly* and publishing *Making Pottery without a Wheel* (1965) with Janice Lovoos and *Decorating Pottery with Clay, Slip and Glaze* (1967). BT

Sources
- F. Carlton Ball and Spencer David, *F. Carlton Ball: Ceramic Works, 1940–1990*, exh. cat. (Tacoma, Wash.: Tacoma Art Museum, 1990).
- Janice Lovoos, "F. Carlton Ball, A California Potter," *American Artist*, June 1964, 50–55, 93–95.

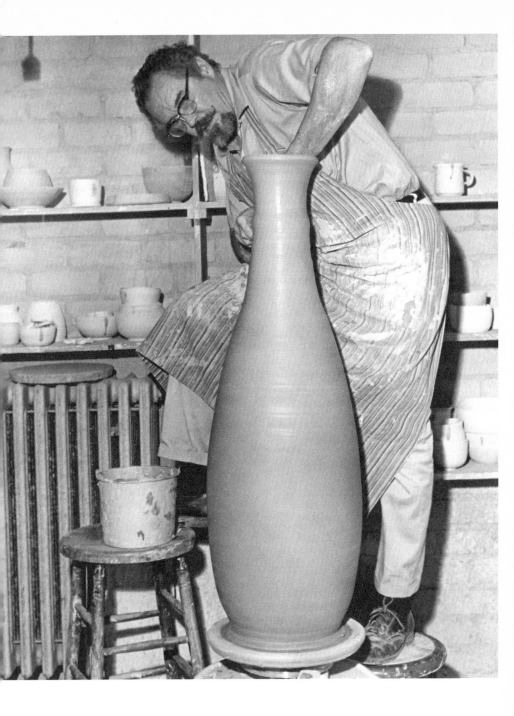

Louella Ballerino
1900–1978

Fashion designer Louella Ballerino incorporated folklore and non-Western motifs into contemporary clothing suited to the relaxed California lifestyle. The Iowa native majored in art and art history at USC and studied textile design with MGM costume designer Andre-Ani. After the onset of the Great Depression, she began selling fashion sketches to dress shops and wholesalers, worked in a custom dress shop, and took courses in pattern making and tailoring at Frank Wiggins Trade School in Los Angeles, where she was soon offered a job teaching fashion design and illustration. In 1938, when her design for a peasant-style dress with a decorative border pattern was rejected, she hired a manufacturer to make the dress out of hopsack. A Hollywood shop owner agreed to let her hang some of the dresses in his window, and their swift sale launched her business. Trips to Mexico and her intensive study of Latin American, Native American, African, Asian, and European folk art in museums and libraries provided the source material for her fashion designs. In addition to the peasant look, Ballerino created some of the first coordinated mother-daughter outfits, and a contract with Oregon-based manufacturer Jantzen from 1946 to 1948 resulted in a successful swimwear and beachwear line in fabrics evocative of exotic locales. As a member of the Affiliated Fashionists of California, Ballerino worked with other women designers to promote "The California Look" nationwide. JMM

Sources
- Louella Ballerino Collection, Doris Stein Research Center, Department of Costume and Textiles, Los Angeles County Museum of Art.
- Beryl Epstein, "Louella Ballerino," in *Fashion Is Our Business* (Freeport, N.Y.: Books for Libraries Press, 1945), 154–70.

Saul Bass
1920–1996

One of the foremost graphic designers of his era, Saul Bass was renowned for his innovations in film title and corporate identity design. Characterized by a reductivist precision, Bass's work used simple, bold graphics to communicate complex ideas and distill the missions of large corporations. Born in New York, Bass supplemented his on-the-job training as a commercial artist with night classes at the Art Students League and Brooklyn College. He came to specialize in trade advertising for film, and in 1946 Buchanan & Company Advertising transferred him to Los Angeles to work with clients in Hollywood. He established his own office in 1952 and only three years later shocked audiences with his radically abstract animated title sequence for Otto Preminger's film *The Man with the Golden Arm*. Partnering with several celebrated directors, including Preminger, Alfred Hitchcock, and Martin Scorsese, Bass created dozens of titles, often in collaboration with his second wife, designer Elaine Bass (b. 1927). Their titles brilliantly expressed the mood and message of each film in a short, metaphorical sequence. In the early 1960s Bass began making short films—many with Elaine—and received an Academy Award for *Why Man Creates* (1968). Films, however, accounted for less than half of the output of Saul Bass & Associates; the majority of work consisted of corporate identity campaigns. In the 1960s Bass developed identity guidelines for international corporations such as Alcoa and Continental Airlines, designing everything from logos to packages to flight attendant uniforms. The firm was renamed Bass/Yager & Associates in 1978 when Herb Yager came on as a financial partner. Other collaborators included illustrator Art Goodman, who worked for Bass for more than thirty years, and sculptor Herb Rosenthal, who worked with Bass on environmental design, including an installation at the 1968 Milan Triennale. ss

Sources
- Saul Bass Papers, Margaret Herrick Library, Academy of Motion Picture Arts and Sciences, Beverly Hills.
- Jennifer Bass and Pat Kirkham, *Saul Bass: A Life in Film and Design* (London: Laurence King, 2011).
- *Idea Archive 01: Saul Bass and Associates* (Nishikicho, Japan: Seibundo Shinkosha, 1979).

Milo Baughman
1923–2003

"A design can be structurally honest . . . even when it gives people what they want and need and will buy," declared furniture designer Milo Baughman.[1] In his long career, the prolific designer opposed what he considered to be the inhospitable forms of high modernism, advocating instead for casual, comfortable furniture that appealed to a broad market. Originally from Goodland, Kansas, Baughman moved to Long Beach as an infant. After serving in World War II, he attended Art Center School and completed his degree at Chouinard Art Institute. While in school, he designed television cabinets and was responsible for upholstery and interior design at Frank Brothers, an influential modern furniture store in Long Beach. Baughman married designer Olga Lee in 1949, and two years later the couple founded Baughman-Lee, a contemporary design shop in Los Angeles that retailed their work and offered decorating services. The collaboration lasted until their divorce around 1954. Baughman continued to design for many local and national furniture companies, including Glenn of California, Pacific Iron Products, and Drexel. The strong, angular lines and metal frames that distinguished his early work remained characteristic of his furniture even as he updated his aesthetic to reflect contemporary trends. In 1953 he began designing modern furniture for North Carolina manufacturer Thayer Coggin, a partnership that lasted for the remainder of his life and resulted in hundreds of products. Baughman left California in 1956 and lived in several cities over the ensuing decades. In 1969 Baughman, who had converted to Mormonism, was named chairman of the Department of Environmental Design at Brigham Young University. ss

1.
Marilyn Hoffman, "California Designer of Furniture Keeps Considerate Eye on Customer."

Sources
· Heather L. Schreckengast, "Milo Baughman: Modern Legend," *Florida Design*, Spring 2003, 74, 76, 78, 80.
· Marilyn Hoffman, "California Designer of Furniture Keeps Considerate Eye on Customer," *Christian Science Monitor*, September 10, 1952.
· James J. Cowen, "Milo Baughman Designs 'California House,'" *Furniture Field*, May 1950, 16.

Olga Lee and Milo Baughman.

Harry Bertoia
1915–1978

Harry Bertoia, a renowned sculptor, graphic artist, and designer of furniture and jewelry, was born Arieto Bertoia in San Lorenzo, Italy. After immigrating to Detroit in 1930, he studied and later taught at Cranbrook Academy of Art, where Charles Eames and Eero Saarinen were instructors. By 1939 Bertoia was teaching metalworking at Cranbrook and experimenting in the print shop; his monotypes—a creative endeavor he continued throughout his life—and his jewelry garnered early recognition. In 1943 Bertoia married Brigitta Valentiner, the daughter of prominent art historian and Los Angeles Museum of History, Science and Art director William Valentiner, and moved to California. While working at the Eames Office in Venice, Bertoia was involved with defense projects and the development of molded-plywood furniture. After leaving the Eameses in 1946, Bertoia made jewelry and monoprints that were shown at the Nierendorf Gallery in New York. His jewelry exploring sculptural form and the play of light on metal was featured in the exhibition *Modern Jewelry under Fifty Dollars* at the Walker Art Center (1948). From 1947 to 1950 Bertoia worked in the publications department at Point Loma Naval Electronics Laboratory in San Diego. During this period he shared a studio with designer Barney Reid and continued to make prints and jewelry, exhibiting with the Allied Craftsmen of San Diego beginning in 1948. He also began making sculpture. Bertoia left California for Pennsylvania in 1950 to develop his iconic wire chairs produced by Knoll Associates. In 1953 he left Knoll to concentrate on welded-metal sculpture, the focus of his work for the rest of his life. JMM

Sources
· Harry Bertoia Papers, 1917–1979, Archives of American Art, Smithsonian Institution.
· Nancy N. Schiffer and Val O. Bertoia, *The World of Bertoia* (Atglen, Pa.: Schiffer, 2003).
· June Kompass Nelson, *Harry Bertoia, Printmaker: Monotypes and Other Monographics* (Detroit: Wayne State University Press, 1988).
· Harry Bertoia, interview by Paul Cummings, June 20, 1972, Archives of American Art, Smithsonian Institution.

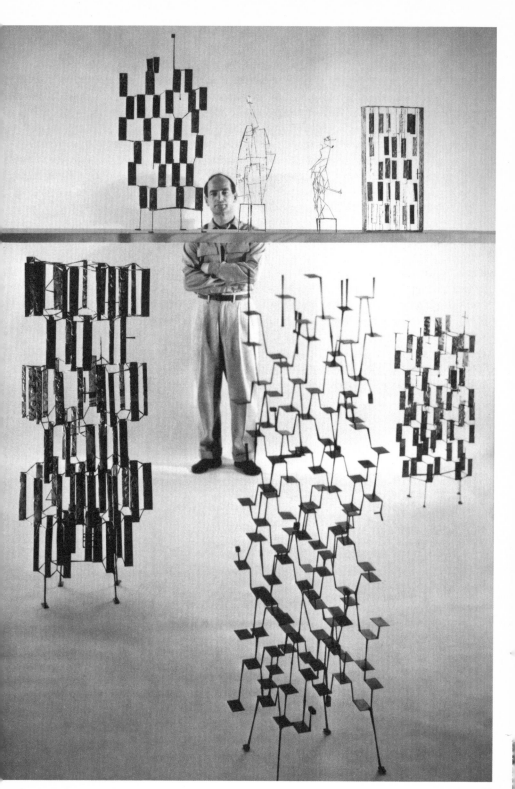

Porter Blanchard
1886–1973

In his long career, silversmith Porter Blanchard created high-end hollowware and flatware that expertly interpreted both historicist and streamlined modern styles. Born in Littleton, Massachusetts, Blanchard hailed from a long line of craftsmen and was trained by his father, silversmith George Porter Blanchard. Lured by the temperate climate, Blanchard arrived in California in 1923 and opened a shop in Burbank. Already a member of the Society of Arts and Crafts, Boston, Blanchard became founding president of the short-lived Arts and Crafts Society of Southern California in 1925. Although he created some exact reproductions, Blanchard often made simplified interpretations of colonial wares, and by the late 1920s had added modern patterns to his line, including several by Kem Weber. Blanchard and his team of craftsmen made complex pieces by hand, but it was their use of machinery for processes such as spinning and polishing that dramatically increased output, allowing Blanchard to sell standardized designs in silver and more affordable pewter at exclusive department stores across the country. In 1933 Blanchard opened a retail shop on Sunset Boulevard that catered to Hollywood clients, among them Joan Crawford and Cary Grant. His work was shown at the Paris International Exposition (1937) and the Golden Gate International Exposition (1939–40), as well as *California Design 9* (1965). Blanchard employed as many as twenty-five craftsmen at his peak, with his best-known apprentices being his sons-in-law Allan Adler and Lewis Wise. Upon Blanchard's death, Wise took over the shop and continued to produce Blanchard's patterns. ss

Sources
· Porter Blanchard Papers, 1914–1983, Archives of American Art, Smithsonian Institution.
· W. Scott Braznell, "Southern California Modernism Engages Colonial New England," *The Magazine Antiques*, July/August 2012, 142–44.
· Leslie Greene Bowman, "Arts and Crafts Silversmiths: Friedell and Blanchard in Southern California," in *Silver in the Golden State*, exh. cat. (Oakland: Oakland Museum, 1986), 41–55.

Industrial designer and engineer Mitchell Bobrick used modern materials and technologie
to create innovative lighting and communication systems. Born in Colorado, Bobrick earned a
BA in aeronautical engineering from Denver University before moving to California in 194
to work for Lockheed Corporation. In the late 1940s he began working as an independent
designer, creating storage cabinets with tubular legs and a popular series of lamps with
two key features: ceramic housings that controlled heat and fiberglass reflectors that
diffused and directed light. Originally sold by General Lighting Company, the line of lamps
was branded Controlight in 1951 and marketed by a small Los Angeles company of the
same name. In about 1960 Bobrick founded Mitchell Bobrick, Inc., a product development
and design firm in Beverly Hills (later in Culver City) that specialized in custom lighting and
electronic telecommunication systems. By 1967 Bobrick had a staff of twenty-one and
a client list that included Lightolier, Sunbeam Lighting Company, the Air Force dental
laboratories, and the architecture firm Skidmore, Owings & Merrill. Contrary to conventional industry practice, Bobrick's firm would create and patent fully developed,
unsolicited designs and present them to potential manufacturers. He explained his unorthodox approach, arguing that designers were ethically obligated to "keep an eye for
a vacuum: for something that falls far short of what it should or could be."[1] ss

1.
Diane Cochrane, "Invention Is the Key," 35.

Sources
· Diane Cochrane, "Invention Is the Key,"
Industrial Design 22 (September 1975): 33–35.
· J. Roger Guilfoyle, "Mitchell Bobrick, Inc.,"
Industrial Design, June 1967, 44–45.

Mitchell Bobrick for Controlight Company, *Controlight* lamp and bookshelf, c. 1949.
LACMA, Purchased with funds provided by Sam and Gracie Miller.

Combining hard-edged graphic lines and lively fields of pattern and color, fashion illustrator Betty Brader developed the visual identity of the trendsetting San Francisco–based specialty-store chain Joseph Magnin. A self-taught artist, Brader was working as an illustrator in Los Angeles in the early 1940s when her distinctive style caught the attention of Magnin's advertising department. Together with advertising director Toni Harley and art director Marget Larsen, Brader defined the store's image through her posters and newspaper advertisements. She preferred to work from live models but wou exaggerate their features and proportions, often using color to emphasize the clothing over the figures. Her slender, stylized bodies created such a recognizable look that her artwork, rather than the company logo, came to dominate the advertisements. Widely praised in advertising and graphic design periodicals, Brader received awards from the Art Directors Club chapters in San Francisco, New York, and Los Angeles. She accepted freelance illustration jobs and worked with other clients—most notably the Neiman Marcus department store in Dallas—but is known primarily for her work at Joseph Magnin, where she remained until shortly before the Magnin family sold the company in 1969. After her departure, she shifted her focus to oil painting, traveling with her husband, artist Frank N. Ashley, to paint portraits and equestrian subjects. The Smithsonian Institution's National Museum of American History holds a large collection of Brader's Joseph Magnin posters. ss

Sources
· Betty Brader-Ashley Papers, Gladys Marcus Library, Fashion Institute of Technology, New York City.
· Study files, Balch Art Research Library, LACMA, DEC.002.

FOLLOW THE LEADER
JOSEPH MAGNIN-CENTURY CITY
OPENS TODAY AT 11 A.M.

come along and join us. jm gets fashion off the ground by starting right off with unbeatable fall clothes and accessories backed up with non-stop service. get going now, we wouldn't want to start without you.

JOSEPH MAGNIN, CENTURY SQUARE, CENTURY CITY 10250 santa monica boulevard between wilshire and beverly glen. open tonight until 9:30; tomorrow 10:00 to 6:00

Betty Brader, Poster for Joseph Magnin department store, 1965.
Archives Center, National Museum of American History, Smithsonian Institution.

Brayton Laguna Pottery
1927–1968

One of the first producers of solid-color dinnerware, Brayton Laguna Pottery is often credited as the originator of the craze for brightly colored pottery that enlivened many tables in Depression-era American homes. Its founder, Durlin E. Brayton (1897–1951), was born in California, graduated from Hollywood High School, studied at the Art Institute of Chicago and Otis Art Institute, and worked as a carpenter before he began making pottery. In 1927 Brayton opened a shop in his home on Pacific Coast Highway in Laguna Beach, which had become a burgeoning artists' colony. He created press-molded earthenware in an impressive array of glowing colors and attracted buyers by displaying the wares in his front yard. In addition to the simple forms of his dinnerware, Brayton sold limited quantities of artware and figurines. The pottery moved to a larger facility in 1938 after Brayton decided to capitalize on the market for mass-produced figurines; the company was the first licensee of ceramic versions of Walt Disney Studios' popular animated characters. Drawing from the artists' colony in Laguna, the company tapped sculptors to model a wide range of collectible figures. From the 1940s figurine production made up the bulk of the firm's business. JMM

Sources
- Jennifer J. Bush, "Pottery Pioneer Laguna's Brayton Ceramics Shop Is Gone, but Its Work Is Far from Forgotten," *Orange County Register*, May 1, 2005.
- Jack Chipman, *Collector's Encyclopedia of California Pottery* (Paducah, Ky.: Collector Books, 1999), 57–58.

Durlin Brayton for Brayton Laguna Pottery, Dinnerware set, c. 1930.
Collection of Bill Stern.

Margaret Bruton
1894–1983
Esther Bruton
1896–1992
Helen Bruton
1898–1985

Artists Margaret, Esther, and Helen Bruton, often referred to collectively as the Bruton sisters, worked as painters, printmakers, sculptors, muralists, and mosaicists. Margaret, the eldest, studied at the Mark Hopkins Institute of Art in San Francisco before winning a scholarship to the Art Students League in New York, where she was a student of Robert Henri and Frank Vincent DuMond. Esther and Helen followed her to the Art Students League, where they learned from several prominent teachers as well, including George Bridgman and Alexander Stirling Calder. The sisters returned to California, and Margaret and Helen continued their studies with painter Armin Hansen in Monterey. All three sisters traveled to Europe in 1925 and took classes at the Académie de la Grande Chaumière in Paris. While they continued to paint, draw, and make prints throughout their entire careers, by the early 1930s they were devoting much of their time to frescoes and mosaics. They often worked on commission, both individually and as collaborators, completing mosaics for Mother's House at the San Francisco Zoo as part of the Public Works of Art Project and the billboard-size colored-plywood relief *Peacemakers* for the Court of the Pacific at the Golden Gate International Exposition (1939–40), where Margaret also showed a relief mosaic. In the late 1930s Margaret became well known for her terrazzo tabletops and plaques favored by renowned decorator Frances Elkins. The sisters settled permanently in Monterey in the 1940s. An exhibition of the mosaics of all three Brutons was held at Gump's Galleries in San Francisco in 1949, and Margaret's work was featured in such exhibitions as *The Arts of Daily Living* (1954), a display organized by Millard Sheets in association with the magazine *House Beautiful* at the Los Angeles County Fair. JMM

Sources
- Sarah Burns, "Fabricating the Modern," in *American Women Modernists: The Legacy of Robert Henri, 1910–1945*, exh. cat. ed. Marian Wardle. (New Brunswick, N.J., and London: Brigham Young University Museum of Art in association with Rutgers University Press, 2005).
- Helen and Margaret Bruton, interview by Lewis Ferbraché, December 4, 1964, Archives of American Art, Smithsonian Institution.
- Dorothy Puccinelli, "The Brutons and How They Grew," *California Arts and Architecture*, October 1940, 18–19, 41.
- Gene Hailey, ed., "Margaret Bruton," *California Art Research* 16, WPA Project 2874, San Francisco, 1936–37, 1–31.

(From left) Helen, Esther, and Margaret Bruton.

Arthur Espenet Carpenter
1920–2006

Furniture maker and wood turner Arthur Espenet Carpenter embodied the ideal of the successful rural craftsman and served as a role model to a generation of woodworkers who sought to live close to nature and support themselves through their craft. His diverse influences—which included designer Charles Eames, Pennsylvania furniture maker Wharton Esherick, and Scandinavian design—shaped his expressive style and pragmatic technique. Born in New York City, Carpenter attended Dartmouth before enlisting in the U.S. Navy in 1942. After the war, he returned to New York. A James Prestini turned-wood bowl exhibited at MoMA inspired him to move to San Francisco in 1948 and teach himself woodturning. Once there he began using his middle name, Espenet, professionally to avoid the pun "Art Carpenter." He soon showed his thin-walled bowls regularly (including at several of MoMA's *Good Design* exhibitions) and sold them through his own retail shop. In 1957 he moved to rural Bolinas, 30 miles north of San Francisco. By the time of his 1959 solo exhibition at the Long Beach Museum of Art, which included only turnings, he was predominantly making furniture with organic shapes and curved lines that epitomized what was later called the California Roundover style. Carpenter rejected purist notions of the handmade, instead embracing construction shortcuts and labor-saving machinery. He produced furniture mainly for residential commissions but also completed some institutional projects, notably for the Mill Valley Library (1966). In 1972 his former apprentice Tom D'Onofrio invited him to cofound the Baulines Craftsman's Guild, an organization that trained craftspeople under a traditional apprenticeship structure. Carpenter eventually taught more than 130 students. His work was shown in many important exhibitions, including the landmark *Woodenworks* show at the Renwick Gallery in Washington, D.C. (1972), which confirmed his place in the canon of his craft. ss

Sources
- Arthur Espenet Carpenter, *Education of a Woodsmith* (n.p.: Bubinga Press, 2010).
- Arthur Espenet Carpenter, interview by Kathleen Hanna, June 20–September 4, 2001, Archives of American Art, Smithsonian Institution.
- Glenn Adamson, "California Dreaming," in *Furniture Studio: The Heart of the Functional Arts*, ed. John Kelsey and Rick Mastelli (Free Union, Va.: Furniture Society, 1999), 32–43.
- Rick Mastelli, "Art Carpenter: The Independent Spirit of the Baulines Craftsman's Guild," *Fine Woodworking*, November/December 1982, 62–68.
- Michael Stone, "The Espenet Style," *American Craft*, June/July 1982, 6–9.

Catalina Clay Products Company
1927–1937

Catalina Clay Products Company, named for the island on which it was founded, was an early producer of the solid-color dinnerware that became common in households in California and across America. When Chicago chewing-gum magnate William Wrigley Jr. (1861–1932) purchased Catalina Island in 1919, he set about transforming it into a resort destination featuring Spanish-style architecture. He hired builder David M. Renton to execute his vision, and they decided to manufacture their own construction materials from clays found on the island. The Tile Factory, established in 1927, soon introduced decorative tile and novelty items. In 1930 a separate pottery plant, the Catalina Clay Products Company, was established for the production of ceramics for home, garden, and table. Available in a range of saturated colors evocative of the island itself, Catalina dinnerware, which from 1936 also included lines in pastel glazes, was manufactured in shapes derived from traditional tablewares as well as modern, Art Deco–inspired forms. As the popularity of "Catalinaware" grew, it became the focus of production. In addition to the shop on the island, the firm opened a wholesale showroom and retail outlet on Olvera Street in downtown Los Angeles, and the products were distributed through department stores across the country. Despite the success of the products, the pottery was not profitable and closed in 1937. Gladding, McBean & Company acquired the use of the Catalina name along with the firm's inventory, molds, and some equipment. JMM

Sources
· Carole Coates, *Catalina Pottery and Tile, 1927–1937* (Atglen, Pa.: Schiffer, 2001).
· James F. Elliot-Bishop, *Franciscan, Catalina, and Other Gladding, McBean Wares* (Atglen, Pa.: Schiffer, 2001).
· Jeannine L. Pedersen and Stacey A. Otte, *The Art of Catalina Clay Products* (Avalon: Catalina Island Museum Society, 2000).

CataLina
CLay
ProDucts

MAKERS of the FAMOUS
CATALINA POTTERY

TILE TOP TABLES

WROUGHT IRON STANDS

LAMPS AND NOVELTIES

- AVALON -

SANTA CATALINA ISLAND

CALIFORNIA

Catalina Clay Products Company catalogue, 1931.

Catalina Sportswear
founded 1907

Swimwear and clothing giant Catalina Sportswear capitalized on innovative design elements and new materials to create stylish and durable apparel, helping to make California the center of the swimwear industry. Founded in Los Angeles as John C. Bentz Knitting Mills, the company's name was changed to Pacific Knitting Mills in 1912, when it began manufacturing wool-knit swimwear to meet the growing demand for fashionable bathing attire. Edgar W. Stewart (1892–1955), who was hired as a salesman in 1912 and promoted to general manager in 1917, became president of the firm in 1928. Renamed Catalina Knitting Mills, the firm was quick to integrate new materials such as the rubber-cored thread Lastex into its products. Catalina attracted a broad following through clever promotion, employing Hollywood stars to generate publicity and even enlisting a group of Hollywood costume designers to co-create a 1946 collection with Catalina head designer Mary Ann DeWeese. The company was a sponsor of the Miss America pageant in the 1940s, outfitting contestants in Catalina suits with the flying fish logo prominently displayed on both hips. Catalina withdrew its sponsorship in 1950 because a Miss America winner refused to pose in a swimsuit, and the company went on to found the Miss USA, Miss Universe, and Miss Teen USA pageants. Julius Kayser & Co. (later Kayser-Roth) purchased Catalina in 1954. Stewart continued to run the company until his death the following year. In 1993 Authentic Fitness acquired Catalina and Cole of California, which by then shared manufacturing facilities in the city of Commerce under the brands' parent company, Taren. JMM

Sources
- Ann T. Kellogg, Amy T. Peterson, Stefani Bay, and Natalie Swindell, *In an Influential Fashion: An Encyclopedia of Nineteenth- and Twentieth-Century Fashion Designers and Retailers Who Transformed Dress* (Westport, Conn.: Greenwood Press, 2002).
- Lena Lenček and Gideon Bosker, *Making Waves: Swimsuits and the Undressing of America* (San Francisco: Chronicle Books, 1989).
- Study files, Balch Art Research Library, LACMA, DEC.002.

Taro Vine

Hand-printed in California on Nylo-nit,

knitted two-way stretch Lastex, Acetate and Nylon for light weight,

fast drying, long wear. $14.95.

For him: Semi-brief trunk in Nylon. $4.95.

by *Catalina*

Write for folder of other Catalina styles, and name of nearest store. Catalina, Inc., Dept. 609, Los Angeles 13, California

CALIFORNIA STYLIST, Vol. XIV, No. 2. Published monthly, 1020 South Main St., Los Angeles 15, California. All rights reserved. 50c a copy, subscription price, United States and possessions $5.00 a year; Canada, Pan American countries and other foreign countries, $8.00. Entered as second class matter, March 8, 1946, at Post Office, Los Angeles 14, under act of March 3, 1879.

Catalina Sportswear advertisement, 1950.

Cole of California's fashionable swimsuits revolutionized the swimwear industry through the use of vibrant colors, figure-conscious design, and association with Hollywood glamour. Fred Cole (1901–1964)—who had had a short career as a silent film actor—launched the swimwear line at West Coast Knitting Mills, his family's company in Vernon that specialized in drop-seat underwear. Swimwear gradually became the mill's main product, and in 1941 the name Cole of California was officially recorded. In 1936 Fred Cole hired Margit Fellegi (1903–1975) as head designer, a position she held until 1972. Born in Missouri, Fellegi attended the Art Institute of Chicago, worked as a professional dancer, and designed costumes for theater and film before opening her own custom salon in Beverly Hills. At Cole she focused on combining fashion with the freedom of movement necessary for swimwear. Matletex, a process by which rigid fabrics are warp-knit to elastic thread to increase their elasticity, was her invention. This technique, along with the introduction of midriff-baring swimsuits and the use of gold lamé and water-resistant velvets, was among Fellegi's many technical and design innovations. During World War II Cole made parachutes under a government contract and designed swimsuits of surplus parachute silk. Adept at spectacular promotion and merchandising, Fred Cole staged elaborate presentations for buyers such as the "Westward to the Sea" campaign in 1946, credited as the California apparel industry's first gala fashion premiere. Partnerships with champion swimmer–turned–actress Esther Williams from 1948 to 1952 and Parisian couturier Christian Dior beginning in 1955 exemplified the company's successful branding strategies. In 1960 Fred Cole sold the company to Kayser-Roth, and Cole of California (along with Catalina Sportswear) went through a succession of corporate parents before being purchased by Authentic Fitness in 1993. JMM

Sources
· Lena Lenček and Gideon Bosker, *Making Waves: Swimsuits and the Undressing of America* (San Francisco: Chronicle Books, 1989).
· "The Cole Show, Starring Margit Fellegi for the 20th Year," *California Stylist*, November 1956, 44–49.

Streamline

beautiful new backsweep . . . in a Lastex swimsuit . . .
from Cole's "Westward to the Sea" beachwear collection

Cole of California advertisement, 1947.

Luther Conover
1913–1993

Self-taught designer and producer Luther Conover made furniture of easy-to-procure materials utilizing simple manufacturing techniques that appealed to budget-conscious consumers furnishing modern homes in the years following World War II. A Chicago native, Conover attended Kenyon College in central Ohio, and later Northwestern University. After serving in the war, he settled in Northern California. Though he had no formal crafts training, Conover was skilled with his hands and learned to design and make furniture—first from salvaged materials, later from available wood and iron. He often employed high school students in his workshop to assist in production. His furniture was prominently featured in the "Pacifica" marketing effort, which promoted home furnishings inspired by the islands of the Pacific Rim, a project spearheaded by Henry Humphrey, former editor of *House and Garden*, and Harry Jackson, owner of Jacksons, a small chain of Bay Area furniture stores. Beginning in the summer of 1948, Conover opened the Trade Fair, a seasonal outdoor market in Sausalito that sold furniture seconds, Heath Ceramics seconds, and local crafts. The Trade Fair expanded each year, becoming a year-round indoor market in 1950. Supplementing local crafts with imported goods, the Trade Fair became a major retailer and tourist attraction. In 1959 Conover purchased the *Berkeley*, a ferryboat that formerly plied the waters of the San Francisco Bay, and operated the Trade Fair from the ferry until 1973. BT

Sources
· "Jackson's Pacifica: One Idea, Many Designers," *House and Garden*, April 1952, 116–31.
· Study files, Balch Art Research Library, LACMA, DEC.002.

Elsie Crawford created imaginative, often whimsical furniture, products, and environments using inventive construction methods, new materials, and playful manipulations of color and scale. Born Elsie Krummeck, Crawford studied at the New York School of Fine and Applied Art and later became an exhibition designer. She met Victor Gruen (né Gruenbaum) while working on the New York World's Fair (1939–40). The two started the firm Gruenbaum & Krummeck and gained recognition for their innovative retail interiors. In 1941 they relocated their practice to Hollywood and soon married. The partnership and marriage lasted until the early 1950s; during this time they forged lasting relationships with many retail clients, designing multiple outlets of the Grayson and Joseph Magnin department stores and the Barton's Bonbonniere candy shops. Crawford went on to build a successful freelance practice in Los Angeles, creating textiles for L. Anton Maix Fabrics, toys, and lighting, among other projects. By the 1960s she was receiving praise for her large-scale environmental designs, including public sculptures (notably a metal dragon for the May Company department store in San Diego's Mission Valley shopping mall), animal-shaped outdoor furniture for Colortime, and several concrete seating and planter designs, the latter in collaboration with her second husband, architect Neil Crawford. Her seating planters for Architectural Fiberglass (see Architectural Pottery), which required a complicated molding process, won the 1968 American Institute of Interior Designers award for advanced research and development. Elsie Crawford's work was shown in every *California Design* exhibition between 1962 and 1976 and in the Museum of Contemporary Crafts' *Plastic as Plastic* exhibition in New York (1968). ss

Sources
· Elsie Crawford Collection, Oakland Museum of California.
· Erika Doering, Rachel Sivitzky, and Rebecca Welz, eds., *Goddess in the Details: Product Design by Women*, exh. cat. (New York: Association of Women Industrial Designers, 1994), 30–31.
· Mary Lou Loper, "Oases for Asphalt Deserts," *Los Angeles Times*, April 18, 1962.
· "The Practical Touch: Gruen and Krummeck," *Designs*, August 1947, 6.

David Cressey
b. 1916

After an early career as a successful studio potter, David Cressey applied his distinctive textured style to production-line ceramic design. The Los Angeles native began studying ceramics with Vivika Heino at USC and continued with Laura Andreson at UCLA (BA, 1954; MA, 1956). His abstract clay assemblages of vessel-like forms earned awards at the *Wichita National Decorative Arts and Ceramics Exhibition* (1961) and the California State Fair (1961, 1962), among other honors. He taught at UCLA and then at Mount Saint Mary's College in Los Angeles, where he was appointed chairman of the art department in 1961. Shortly afterward, he left teaching to serve as the first artist-in-residence at Architectural Pottery. Cressey created customizable designs for planters, sculpture, sand urns, tiles, and screen walls by applying textured patterns and earthy glazes by hand to cast forms. His wife, artist Donna Cressey (b. 1931), assisted with the hand finishing. A company catalogue touted the economy of these techniques, promising "a one-of-a-kind concept within the reality of commercial budgets and time schedules."[1] Made of a durable stoneware body developed by the artist, Cressey's first collection received the 1964 International Design Award from the American Institute of Interior Designers and was exhibited in *California Design 9* (1965). In 1966 his residency at Architectural Pottery became a permanent position, and his line, which had broken new ground by casting textured stoneware, was renamed the Pro/Artisan Collection. Cressey remained at the firm until 1976, managing production, developing new clay and glaze technologies, and eventually rising to vice president at the parent company, Group Artec. From 1976 to 1987 he was president of Earthgender Ceramics, a producer of ceramic giftware, planters, and lamps. ss

1.
Artist-in-Residence Program, vol. 1, cat.
(Los Angeles: Architectural Pottery, 1963).

Sources
· *Artist-in-Residence Program*, vol. 1, cat.
  (Los Angeles: Architectural Pottery, 1963), in
  the Max and Rita Lawrence, Architectural Pottery
  Records (Collection 1587), Box 4, Folder 23,
  Department of Special Collections, Charles E. Young
  Research Library, University of California,
  Los Angeles.
· Betje Howell, "David Cressey: Potter, Sculptor,
  and Art Instructor," *Creative Crafts*, July/August
  1962, 12–17.
· Study files, Balch Art Research Library, LACMA,
  DEC.002.

Louis Danziger
b. 1923

Graphic designer Louis Danziger uses visual metaphor to convey complex ideas, often building his imagery from precisely layered, deliberately cropped photographs. Born in New York City, Danziger moved to Los Angeles after serving in World War II. His studies with Alvin Lustig at Art Center School (1946–47) and at the California School of Art in Los Angeles (c. 1948–49) and with Alexey Brodovitch at the New School of Social Research in New York (1948) helped foster his commitment to modern ideas as well as his playful experimentation. Opening a freelance practice in 1949, Danziger struggled to find clients who accepted modern design. His early accounts—including his first client, General Lighting Company—were in design-related fields such as furnishings and art supplies. His interest in technology would later attract System Development Corporation, Clinton Laboratories, and other scientific companies. Danziger developed long-standing relationships with LACMA (late 1950s–80) and the oil company ARCO (1978–85). His work regularly won recognition from the AIGA, the Art Directors Club of Los Angeles, and *Graphis* magazine, among others. In the late 1960s Danziger reduced his client load in order to focus on teaching. As director of the graphic design program at the California Institute of the Arts, Danziger introduced students to diverse graphic traditions, pioneering a course in graphic design history and recruiting avant-garde designers for the faculty. Over the course of his long career, Danziger taught at Art Center School (1956–60) and at its successor institution, Art Center College of Design (1986–present), at California Institute of the Arts (1963–87), and at Harvard University (summers between 1978 and 1988). ss

Sources
- Louis Danziger Collection, Wallace Library, Archives and Special Collections, Rochester Institute of Technology.
- Philip B. Meggs, "Notes on a Grand Master," *Print*, September/October 1990, 66–79.
- Henri Hillebrand, ed., *Graphic Designers in the USA*, vol. 1 (New York: Universe Books, 1971), 6–35.

Douglas Deeds
b. 1937

Industrial designer Douglas Deeds embraced the malleable properties of synthetic materials, using plastics to create sculptural, space age–inspired furniture and products. Deeds grew up in San Diego and began experimenting with fiberglass to make surfboards while still in junior high school. After attending Pomona College (BA, 1959), he took graduate courses in design at Pratt Institute in New York (1959–60) and earned a degree in industrial design at Syracuse University (MID, 1961). He founded Deeds Design Associates after returning to San Diego in 1962. From the early 1960s to the mid-1970s Deeds served as director of design at Architectural Fiberglass (see Architectural Pottery), where he developed futuristic outdoor and street furniture and office workstations, among other projects. He used synthetics in his designs for other clients as well, including vinyl lighting for Los Angeles–based Peter Pepper Products and molded polyethylene furniture for the plastics division of Gould Inc. of Milwaukee. Deeds believed that plastics enabled designers to rethink traditional design problems such as seating and shelter without the structural limitations of natural materials. In 1968 Deeds built a room out of sprayed polyurethane foam for the exhibition *Plastic as Plastic* at the Museum of Contemporary Crafts in New York; this highly publicized installation was expanded at the Smithsonian the following year. An early proponent of reusing discarded materials to promote environmental awareness, Deeds built several pieces of furniture out of steel cans for himself in the early 1960s. He was the recipient of the Alcoa Ventures in Design Award (1969), and his work was selected for *California Design 8* through *California Design 11* (1962–1971) and several *Industrial Design* annual reviews, as well as the traveling U.S. Information Agency exhibition *The Need to Recycle* (1972). ss

Sources
· Max and Rita Lawrence, Architectural Pottery Records (Collection 1587), Department of Special Collections, Charles E. Young Research Library, University of California, Los Angeles.
· Dan MacMasters, "Douglas Deeds, 'Call Me a Problem Solver,'" *Los Angeles Times*, May 17, 1977.
· "Designers in California: Deeds Design Associates/Industrial Design," *Industrial Design*, June 1972, 40–41.
· Study files, Balch Art Research Library, LACMA, DEC.002.

Rupert Deese
1924–2010

Ceramic designer and studio potter Rupert "Rummy" Deese made elegant, utilitarian vessels for daily living and was an important member of Claremont's vibrant artistic community. Born in Guam to a military family, he served in World War II and subsequently enrolled at Pomona College, majoring in ceramics (BA, 1950). As a student at Claremont Graduate School (MFA, 1957), Deese studied with Richard B. Petterson. From 1950 until his retirement in 2005 he shared a studio with fellow potter Harrison McIntosh. First located in Claremont, the studio moved in 1958 to a location adjacent to McIntosh's home in nearby Padua Hills. Though Deese and McIntosh shared materials and equipment, including the same clay body until approximately 1954, their working methods and output were different. Deese employed a smooth, dark brown stoneware body, used an array of glazes evocative of California terrain, and created a subtle, muted effect by revealing much of the clay surface. In the early 1950s he produced a line of slip-cast table accessories. In 1964 Millard Sheets recruited Deese to the Franciscan division of Interpace Ceramics (see Gladding, McBean & Company), where he designed dinnerware until 1983. He continued to work in the studio after hours and also taught art at Mount San Antonio College in Walnut from 1957 to 1971. Recognition for his work included a purchase prize at the Everson Museum of Art's *XXI Ceramic National Exhibition* (1960), appearances in several *California Design* and Los Angeles County Fair exhibitions, and a one-man show at the Chinati Foundation (1997). JMM

Sources
- Claire Noland, "Rupert J. Deese Dies at 85; Claremont Artist Created Functional Pottery," *Los Angeles Times*, July 27, 2010.
- Harrison McIntosh, interview by Mary MacNaughton, February 24–March 4, 1999, Archives of American Art, Smithsonian Institution.
- Study files, Balch Art Research Library, LACMA, DEC.002.

Margaret De Patta
1903–1964

A leading figure in modern jewelry design nationwide and a central member of the circle of Bay Area metal craftspeople, Margaret De Patta explored nonobjective concepts of space and transparency in her work. De Patta was steeped in Bauhaus and Constructivist principles, and her jewelry was characterized by an interest in structural form, abstraction, and kinetic movement, as well as the use of nontraditional materials such as rutilated crystals, found minerals, and semiprecious stones. Born Margaret Strong in Tacoma, Washington, she studied painting and sculpture at several art schools in California and New York before settling in 1929 in San Francisco, where she began to study metalworking. Her earliest work featured ancient Egyptian, pre-Columbian, and Etruscan motifs. By 1936 she was operating a workshop out of her home and selling her wares at the esteemed craft shop Amberg-Hirth. Her studies with László Moholy-Nagy at the School of Design in Chicago (formerly the New Bauhaus, now the Institute of Design) in 1940–41 clarified her approach to spatial and structural problems. By 1946 demand for her jewelry had driven up prices, and in a move to make the work more affordable, she designed a line of cast jewelry produced by Designs Contemporary, a business run by her fourth husband, Eugene Bielawski. De Patta found the demands of the production business onerous, and after about ten years she returned to making solely handcrafted jewelry. A founder of the Metal Arts Guild in San Francisco and the Designer-Craftsmen of California, De Patta was featured in numerous exhibitions and was the subject of retrospectives at the Oakland Museum in 1976 and 2012. JMM

Sources
- Margaret De Patta Papers, 1944–2000, Archives of American Art, Smithsonian Institution.
- Ursula Ilse-Neuman and Julie M. Muñiz, *Space, Light, Structure: The Jewelry of Margaret De Patta*, exh. cat. (New York and Oakland: Museum of Arts & Design and Oakland Museum of California, 2012).
- *The Jewelry of Margaret De Patta: A Retrospective Exhibition*, exh. cat. (Oakland: Oakland Museum, 1976).

Mary Ann DeWeese
1913–1993

Appliquéd swimsuits and matching his-and-hers swimwear and sportswear are among the fashion firsts credited to Mary Ann DeWeese. The Kansas-born designer worked for Los Angeles Knitting Mills beginning in the 1930s and created sportswear for Sandeze before joining Catalina Knitting Mills (see Catalina Sportswear), where she became a highly acclaimed designer known for her playful, well-constructed fashions. One of her many successful endeavors, the matching *Sweethearts in Swimsuits* line for men and women in the 1940s, helped establish her reputation for innovation at Catalina. In 1951 she founded her own company in Los Angeles, DeWeese Designs, which produced sportswear and swimwear offering exceptional fit and construction. Her sundresses and loungewear were particularly successful, and she continued to use texture in unique ways and to introduce useful innovations such as the stretch strap for clothing and swimwear. DeWeese Designs remained in operation into the 1980s. JMM

Sources
· Study files, Balch Art Research Library, LACMA, DEC.002.

Carlos Diniz
1928–2001

Architectural delineator Carlos Diniz played an important and specialized role in the production of modern architecture. With his eloquent renderings, Diniz translated the architect's often exceedingly technical vision of a building into a format understood by clients, developers, and the general public. He depicted buildings as they would be lived in and experienced, capturing the color and texture of everyday life. He found the most compelling perspective, added lush landscaping, and filled his drawings with people and alluring accessories. Diniz studied industrial design and architecture at Art Center School and, like many Los Angeles designers and architects of his generation, began his career in the office of Victor Gruen, where he met many future collaborators and clients, including graphic designer Frederick A. Usher Jr. and architects Cesar Pelli and Frank Gehry. He established his architectural rendering firm in 1957 and worked for many well-known architects, including Minoru Yamasaki; Skidmore, Owings & Merrill; Craig Ellwood; and Welton Becket. Cultivating a specialty in the depiction of large-scale commercial structures, Diniz delineated such notable buildings as the Century Plaza Hotel in Los Angeles (Yamasaki, 1966), the World Trade Center in New York City (Yamasaki, 1973), and Faneuil Hall Marketplace in Boston (James Rouse and Benjamin Thompson, 1976). BT

Sources
- Nicholas Olsberg, "For and Against the Modern," *Modernism*, Winter 2008–9, 34–43.
- Carlos Diniz and Frederick A. Usher, *Building Illusion: The Work of Carlos Diniz* (Tokyo: Process Architecture, 1992).

Henry Dreyfuss
1904–1972

Creator of modern icons such as the Bell model 500 telephone (1949) and the Honeywell Round thermostat (1953), Henry Dreyfuss was a distinguished industrial designer known for his commitment to human factors, or ergonomics, the science of applying anatomical research to maximize the comfort and utility of his designs. The results of his research were published in the landmark manual *The Measure of Man* (1960). Dreyfuss attended the Ethical Culture School's Arts High School in his native New York City. Upon graduation in 1922, he studied set design with Norman Bel Geddes, another pioneer of industrial design. Dreyfuss founded his eponymous firm in 1928 in New York. Beginning about 1944, he worked primarily out of a second office in Pasadena, permanently relocating there in 1945. Dreyfuss continued to manage his New York office—still the firm's primary location—through daily air-mail exchanges and frequent trips east, where he kept a suite across the street at the Plaza Hotel. The Pasadena branch served important clients across the country, including Polaroid, John Deere, Convair, and Lockheed. This office employed fewer than ten people but included several of the firm's key designers, including business partner William F. H. "Bill" Purcell, James Conner, Niels Diffrient, Strother MacMinn, and Chuck Pelly. Conner and Diffrient joined Purcell as partners when the firm reorganized around 1967, forming Henry Dreyfuss and Associates. The Pasadena branch closed in 1969 when Dreyfuss retired to work on *Symbol Sourcebook* with his wife and business manager, Doris Marks (1903–1972). Many of the employees relocated to the New York office. ss

Sources
· Henry Dreyfuss Collection, 1927–1972, Cooper-Hewitt Design Archive, Smithsonian Institution.
· Russell Flinchum, *Henry Dreyfuss, Industrial Designer: The Man in the Brown Suit*, exh. cat. (New York: Cooper Hewitt National Design Museum; New York: Rizzoli, 1997).

The leading proponent of a baroque, Hollywood-influenced style, Tony Duquette designe fantastical domestic and retail interiors, sets and costumes for theater and film, and jewelry. He constructed these elaborate settings from both objects of luxury and commc materials such as papier-mâché and plastic, often with coral, antlers, crystals, and mirroi as accents. Raised in Michigan, Duquette returned to his native Los Angeles to attend Chouinard Art Institute around 1933. The ambitious young designer quit school to create promotional displays for J. W. Robinson's and Bullock's department stores as well as freelance furniture and accessories for James Pendleton, William Haines, and other prominent tastemakers. Duquette's mentor, influential decorator Elsie de Wolfe, intro-duced him to major clients and helped him secure an exhibition at the Pavillon de Marsar a part of the Louvre complex, in 1951. In the 1940s he began long-standing collaboration: with director Vincente Minnelli and costume designer Gilbert Adrian, designing opulent sets and costumes for the films *Ziegfeld Follies* (1945) and *Kismet* (1955), as well as a theatrical production of *Camelot*, for which Duquette and Adrian won a Tony Award (1961). Duquette saw his unrestrained style as a spiritual antidote to the sterility of much modern design, and his passionate vision appealed to his devoted clients, such as Mary Pickford, Doris Duke, and Elizabeth Arden. Duquette lived his own style: for his numerou: properties—which included his Beverly Hills home, Dawnridge; a house in San Francisco and Sortilegium, a 170-acre estate in Malibu—he created fanciful spaces and landscapes filled with his signature lavish decoration, exotic materials, and Asian-inspired architec-tural elements. A revival of interest in his work in the late 1990s led to commissions from Oscar de la Renta and Gucci. ss

Sources
· Hutton Wilkinson, *More Is More: Tony Duquette*
(New York: Abrams, 2009).
· Wendy Goodman and Hutton Wilkinson,
Tony Duquette (New York: Abrams, 2007).

Charles Eames
1907–1978
Ray Eames
1912–1988

The most influential California designers of the twentieth century, with many iconic designs still in production today, Charles and Ray Eames had an impact on millions through their furniture, films, exhibitions, and other projects. Born in St. Louis, Charles studied architecture at Washington University. In 1938 Eliel Saarinen invited him to the Cranbrook Academy of Art in Bloomfield Hills, Michigan, where he rose swiftly to become head of the industrial design department. With Eliel's son Eero, Charles submitted designs to MoMA's Organic Design in Home Furnishings competition in 1940, for which they won first prize for their laminated-wood living-room seating and case goods. Charles Eames and Ray Kaiser met at Cranbrook in 1940, where Ray was a student. Born in Sacramento, she had studied painting in New York City with Hans Hofmann and was familiar with avant-garde developments in art, dance, and film. Charles and Ray married in June 1941 and immediately moved to Los Angeles. They befriended modern architecture advocate John Entenza, who turned the magazine *Arts and Architecture* into an influential forum for contemporary art, architecture, and design; Ray designed several covers for the magazine. Charles and Ray designed their celebrated home and studio in Pacific Palisades (1949), which was part of the magazine's Case Study House program. During World War II the Eameses continued the molded-plywood experiments begun at Cranbrook, developing a leg splint for the U.S. Navy and other products. After the war, they set up the Molded Plywood Division of Evans Products Company to produce furniture.

Continued on p. 90

Ray and Charles Eames with prototypes for MoMA's Low-Cost Furniture Competition, 1948.

Distribution was handled by the Michigan-based Herman Miller Furniture Company, and production soon moved to the Michigan plant. Thus began an extremely productive relationship in which Herman Miller made dozens of Eames designs, many in new materials such as molded plywood and fiberglass. The Eames Office, located at 901 Washington Boulevard in Venice, employed many important designers who would go on to become innovators in their chosen fields, including Don Albinson, Harry Bertoia, Charles Kratka, Herbert Matter, Deborah Sussman, Frederick A. Usher Jr., and many others. Prolific filmmakers, the Eameses viewed the medium as a way to explain complex ideas, which often originated in problems explored in their office. Of their more than 125 films, some of the most influential were *Glimpses of the USA*, a multiscreen presentation at the American National Exhibition in Moscow (1959), and *Powers of Ten* (1968). They also developed exhibitions for museums and world's fairs on such diverse topics as mathematics and American history, often commissioned or sponsored by corporate or government clients. They had an ongoing relationship with India, creating several films about the country and producing *The India Report* at the invitation of Prime Minister Jawaharlal Nehru in 1958. An analysis of that country's design culture, the report recommended the creation of what became the National Institute of Design, a center for education and research. While Charles and Ray probably would not have described themselves as California designers because of their international connections and clientele, the commercial success of their designs in all media meant that these products of California were experienced and used throughout the world. BT

Sources
· The Work of Charles and Ray Eames Collection, Library of Congress.
· Marilyn Neuhart, *The Story of Eames Furniture* (Berlin: Gestalten, 2010).
· Eames Demetrios, *An Eames Primer* (New York: Universe Publishing, 2001).
· Donald Albrecht, ed., *The Work of Charles and Ray Eames: A Legacy of Invention* (New York: Abrams, 1997).
· Pat Kirkham, *Charles and Ray Eames: Designers of the Twentieth Century* (Cambridge, Mass.: MIT Press, 1995).
· John Neuhart, Marilyn Neuhart, and Ray Eames, *Eames Design* (New York: Abrams, 1989).

Ray and Charles Eames photographing a scale model of the *Mathematica* exhibition, c. 1960.

Claire Falkenstein
1908–1997

Internationally acclaimed artist Claire Falkenstein worked on scales from miniscule to monumental in an astonishingly diverse oeuvre that included sculpture, jewelry, painting, printmaking, and other media. Originally from Coos Bay, Oregon, Falkenstein graduated from the University of California, Berkeley, in 1930 with a major in art and minors in philosophy and anthropology. Prior to graduating, she received her first solo art exhibition at East-West Gallery in San Francisco. She studied at Mills College with modernist sculptor Alexander Archipenko in 1933 and spent the 1930s and 1940s teaching at several Bay Area arts institutions while creating and exhibiting her own work, including a relief for the Golden Gate International Exposition (1939–40). In preparing to receive an award for a wall-covering design from the American Institute of Decorators in 1948, Falkenstein made a hatpin to wear. This marked the beginning of an interest in jewelry that, in addition to helping her explore metalworking techniques, was related visually and conceptually to her large forged sculptures. Falkenstein moved to Paris in 1950 and lived in Europe for the next thirteen years. There her interest in sculptural space manifested in a number of recurring themes in her sculpture, including the never-ending screen, topological and lattice structures, and kinetic movement. In 1954 she began to incorporate glass into her metalwork, which she used in several prominent commissions, including the gates for the Peggy Guggenheim Collection in Venice, Italy (1961), and the windows and doors of St. Basil Catholic Church in Los Angeles (1969). The artist moved to Venice, California, in 1963, where she lived and worked until her death in 1997, the same year the Fresno Art Museum presented a retrospective exhibition of her work. JMM

Sources
- Claire Falkenstein Papers, c. 1914–1997, Archives of American Art, Smithsonian Institution.
- *Claire Falkenstein*, exh. cat., essays by Susan M. Anderson, Michael Duncan, and Maren Henderson (Los Angeles: Falkenstein Foundation, 2012).
- *The Modernist Jewelry of Claire Falkenstein*, exh. cat., introduction by Harold B. Nelson, essay by Maren Henderson (Long Beach: Long Beach Museum of Art, 2004).
- Claire Falkenstein, interview by Paul Karlstrom, March 2–21, 1995, Archives of American Art, Smithsonian Institution.
- Noreen Larinde, "Claire Falkenstein," *Woman's Art Journal* 1, no. 1 (Spring/Summer 1980): 50–55.

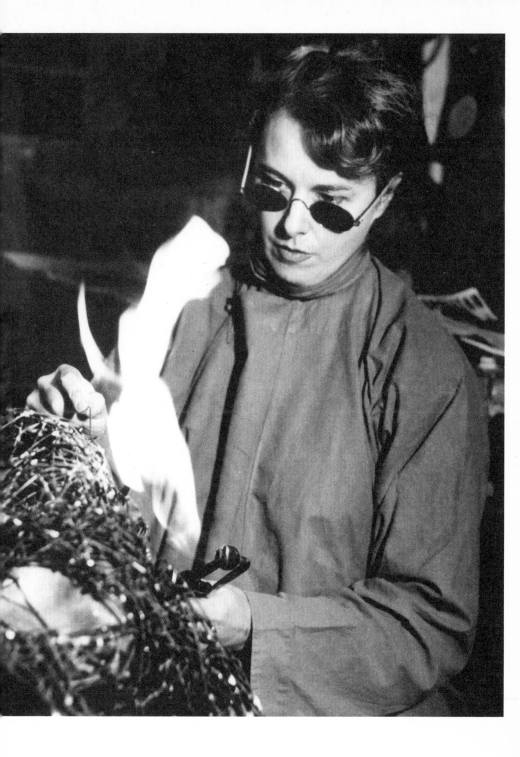

Arline Fisch
b. 1931

A leader among California jewelers, Arline Fisch is renowned for the broad range of styles, materials, and techniques she employed, as well as the development of new jewelry types. Born in Brooklyn, Fisch studied art at Skidmore College in upstate New York and at the University of Illinois. In 1961 she was appointed professor at San Diego State University, where she taught jewelry and metalsmithing until 1999. She was awarded a Fulbright grant to study at the Kunsthåndværkerskolen (School of Arts and Crafts) in Denmark from 1956 to 1957, where she acquired the metalworking techniques that would become the core of her future work. Subsequent travel in Europe and Central America allowed her to intensively research collections of jewelry and metalwork, which informed her designs. Fisch's innovations include the application of fiber techniques such as weaving and knitting to metal—described in her book *Textile Techniques in Metal* (1975)—and the large body ornaments she began to create in the mid-1960s, redefining the genre and creating new categories of jewelry. She has used gold, enamel, pearls, ivory, feathers, and agate in her pieces, and has worked in aluminum and ColorCore laminate. Fisch has been an active member of the American Craft Council and World Crafts Council, and was a founding member of the Society of North American Goldsmiths. Her work has been shown in dozens of museum and gallery exhibitions since 1955, and she has received several solo shows, including one at the Pasadena Art Museum (1962) and the traveling retrospective *Elegant Fantasy: The Jewelry of Arline Fisch* (2000). BT

Sources
- Arline M. Fisch Papers, Archives of American Art, Smithsonian Institution.
- Arline M. Fisch, David Revere McFadden, San Diego Historical Society et al., *Elegant Fantasy: The Jewelry of Arline Fisch*, exh. cat. (San Diego: San Diego Historical Society; Stuttgart: Arnoldsche, 1999).

John Follis
1923–1994

Pasadena-born designer John Follis worked in an astounding range of media, designing ceramic planters, furniture, and exhibits, and by the 1970s had become a leader in the burgeoning field of environmental graphics. After serving in World War II, Follis studied with Alvin Lustig, first at Art Center School (1947–48) and then at the California School of Art in Los Angeles. There Follis and classmate Rex Goode (1925–2000) responded to a challenge from instructor La Gardo Tackett to market ceramic planters that their class designed for an assignment. With some modifications, the planters became the first line produced by the company Architectural Pottery, which Follis and Goode founded with Max and Rita Lawrence in 1950. Follis remained involved with the firm through the early 1960s, designing both the award-winning logo and the first planters for the Architectural Fiberglass division. During this time he also worked as an interior designer for architect Welton Becket and was responsible for dozens of covers and layouts for the magazines *Arts and Architecture* and *Everyday Art*. Follis continued to collaborate with Goode, establishing a firm that specialized in exhibition, three-dimensional, and graphic design; the pair also opened the modern furnishings store Heron-Teak in Pasadena. In 1960 Follis and Frederick A. Usher Jr. formed Usher-Follis, a general design firm that became John Follis & Associates in 1964. A pioneer in the field of environmental signage, Follis codified his functional yet elegant approach in the influential book *Architectural Signing and Graphics* (1979), coauthored with Dave Hammer. His way-finding systems helped users navigate such complex sites as ARCO Plaza in downtown L.A. (c. 1971) and the San Diego Wild Animal Park (1972–73), as well as the identity and signage for the Los Angeles Bicentennial (1980). ss

Sources
· *20 Outstanding L.A. Designers*, directed by Archie Boston (1986; Los Angeles: Archie Boston Graphic Design, 2008), DVD.
· Marshall Berges, "Home Q&A: June and John Follis," *Los Angeles Times*, April 8, 1979.
· Study files, LACMA, Balch Art Research Library, DEC.002.

John Follis (center) with Art Center College of Design students, c. 1976.

Danny Ho Fong
1915–1992
Miller Yee Fong
b. 1941

Self-taught designer Danny Ho Fong transformed Fong Brothers Company, his family's Southeast Asian import business, with a successful line of modern rattan patio furniture and housewares characterized by simple lines and elegantly curving forms. His son Miller Yee Fong continued this legacy with his own rattan furniture designs. Born Ho Ming Fong in China, Danny settled in the Los Angeles area in the late 1930s and joined the family business. When the rise of the Communist Party cut off trade with China in 1949, the company shifted its focus to rattan furniture made in British Hong Kong. To distinguish h company's wares from those of his competitors, Danny began developing his own design in 1952, hiring workers in Hong Kong to shape the pliable Indonesian vine into intricate updates of traditional styles as well as airy, cantilevered forms. These were attached to iron frames that were shipped to Asia from the United States. An adept promoter, he began using the trade name Tropi-Cal in 1954, a moniker that linked the exotic material with L.A.'s sunny climate and outdoor lifestyle. Fong sold his furniture in upscale stores, received regular coverage in the *Los Angeles Times Home* magazine and *House Beautifu* and in 1966 won the International Design Award from the American Institute of Interior Designers for his *Mold* chair. Danny's success paved the way for his son Miller, who bega designing for the company in his early twenties. Trained as an architect at USC (B.Arch, 1964), Miller absorbed the modern tenets of his teachers, architects Donald Hensman ar Conrad Buff, building several homes in Pasadena for his extended family. Like his father, he made his greatest impact in rattan, using iron frames to create dramatically curved forms, most notably in his *Lotus* chair, featured in *California Design 10* (1968). Under the helm of Miller and his brother Theodore, Fong Brothers began to concentrate on hospitality commissions in the late 1960s and switched to using more durable synthetic rattan. Still family owned today, the company continues to produce outdoor furniture, including reissues of their classic designs. ss

Sources
· Rita Reif, "Designed in the U.S., Made in Hong Kong," *New York Times*, March 5, 1971.
· Dan MacMasters, "Danny Ho Fong," *Los Angeles Times*, March 15, 1970.
· Study files, Balch Art Research Library, LACMA, DEC.002.

Danny Ho Fong in his *Empress* chair.

Paul T. Frankl
1886–1958

A leading tastemaker and advocate for modern American design, Paul T. Frankl was born in Vienna and studied architecture in Europe before traveling throughout the United States and Japan in 1914. Marooned in New York City during World War I, he returned to Austria in 1917 but came back to New York in 1921, where he established an interior design firm and became well known for his *Skyscraper* furniture, which, with its stepped profile, evoked the city's skyline and the glamour of the Jazz Age. In the summer of 1934 he moved to Los Angeles to teach at Chouinard Art Institute and soon opened Frankl Galleries, a showroom that offered interior design services and retailed his furniture and other products. His interior design practice flourished as he received commissions from many of Hollywood's elite, including Fred Astaire, Katharine Hepburn, and Alfred Hitchcock. In addition to his custom work, Frankl wanted to design furniture for mass production. Admiring the aesthetics and materials he had seen in Asia, he created a line of rattan furniture that was manufactured in the Philippines in the late 1930s, sparking a rattan craze that resulted in countless imitations and knockoffs. Beginning in 1949 he produced dozens of designs for the Grand Rapids, Michigan, manufacturer Johnson Furniture Company, many of which were based on custom models for architect Cliff May. Frankl was a gifted self-promoter and the subject of countless articles in shelter and industry magazines. He also lectured frequently and wrote several books on his design philosophy, including *New Dimensions* (1928) and *Space for Living* (1938). BT

Sources
· Christopher Long, *Paul T. Frankl and Modern American Design* (New Haven, Conn.: Yale University Press, 2007).

Kenji Fujita
1921–2012

Born in Los Angeles to parents of Japanese descent, Kenji Fujita designed ceramic wares for the modern table. He displayed artistic talent from an early age and, after graduating from high school, worked for a firm that created window displays in downtown Los Angeles. After the United States entered World War II, Fujita and his family were sent to the Poston War Relocation Center in Yuma County, Arizona, in May 1942, where they were interned for three and a half years. During this period one of his activities was producing posters used throughout the camp. After the war, Fujita attended Frank Wiggins Trade School for a few semesters. In the late 1940s he began working with La Gardo Tackett to design modern ceramic tablewares that were slip cast in Tackett's workshop in Topanga Canyon and, later, in Santa Monica. The vessels included storage jars, bowls, pitchers, and cruets, some of which were in abstracted animal shapes. He also created sleek porcelain vessels for the distributor Freeman Lederman. In the late 1950s Fujita changed careers to work in the more lucrative aerospace field. As an employee of North American Aviation and its successor companies, he served as a technical illustrator, depicting aircraft and spacecraft for internal and promotional purposes until his retirement in the 1990s. BT

Sources
- Study files, Balch Art Research Library, LACMA, DEC.002.

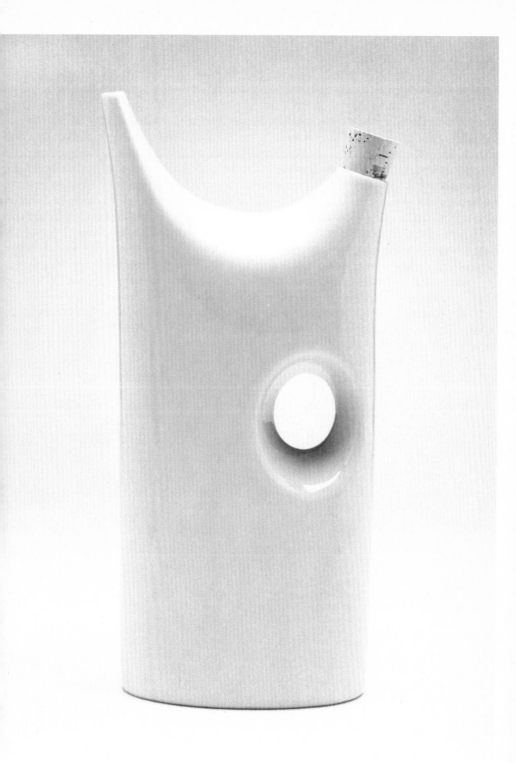

Kenji Fujita, Condiment bottle, c. 1960. LACMA, Gift of Emily Tigerman.

Rudi Gernreich
1922–1985

Famous for his boldly graphic and animal-print patterns, striking combinations of saturated colors, and unorthodox materials, visionary designer Rudi Gernreich introduced many new style trends and repeatedly challenged the conventions of fashion. Born in Vienna to a progressive family of Jewish descent, he fled the growing Nazi threat in 1938, arriving in Los Angeles on the same ship as Gertrud and Otto Natzler. Gernreich enrolled at Los Angeles City College and attended Art Center School in the early 1940s. For most of that decade he studied and performed with the Lester Horton Dance Theater and designed costumes for film and dance. He unveiled his first clothing line in 1948, but lack of experience in the fashion industry forestalled production of his designs. It was not until 1951, when Gernreich partnered with sportswear manufacturer Walter Bass, that his career and reputation as an avant-garde designer were established. In 1954 he created curve-hugging knit swimsuits for Westwood Knitting Mills that were distinct from the structured suits popular at the time. Gernreich founded his own company in 1960 to produce a range of fashions from sportswear to formal attire. In his ongoing effort to liberate women's bodies from what he felt were the physical constraints of conventional clothing, he introduced the notorious topless swimsuit in 1964. It became an international sensation and attracted the controversy and media coverage typically provoked by his radical fashions. Gernreich was deeply committed to social causes and was one of the founding members of the Mattachine Society, an early advocacy organization for gay rights founded in Los Angeles in 1950. He was the recipient of multiple Coty awards and was featured on the cover of *Time* magazine in 1967. After 1970 Gernreich designed clothing collections with military and unisex themes and created several lines of home accessories for such companies as Lily of France and Knoll International. JMM

Sources
- Rudi Gernreich and the Institute of Contemporary Art, *Rudi Gernreich: Fashion Will Go Out of Fashion*, exh. cat. (Philadelphia: Institute of Contemporary Art, University of Pennsylvania, 2001).
- Peggy Moffitt and William Claxton, *The Rudi Gernreich Book* (New York: Rizzoli, 1991).

Cedric Gibbons
1890–1960

Recipient of eleven Academy Awards, Cedric Gibbons was responsible for elevating art direction to a respected profession in the film industry. The facts of Gibbons's early life and career are murky (his biography was enhanced by studio publicists). What is known is that he was originally from Brooklyn, studied at the Art Students League of New York, and entered his father's architecture practice as a draftsman. He began his film career as an apprentice to set designer and artist Hugo Ballin, first with Edison Studios and later with Goldwyn Picture Corp. Gibbons was an early advocate of three-dimensional set design—painted backdrops were the norm around 1915—and earned a reputation for insisting on authenticity and good taste. He relocated to Los Angeles in 1919 to work at Goldwyn's Culver City studio. Goldwyn merged with Metro Pictures and Louis B. Mayer Productions to form MGM in 1924, and Gibbons served as head of the MGM art department until his retirement in 1956, organizing it into a hierarchy of specialists and unit art directors who reported to him. His contract stipulated that he receive screen credit for every film the studio released, regardless of the extent of his personal involvement. From the late 1920s into the 1930s Gibbons and costume designer Gilbert Adrian brought a luxurious, streamlined aesthetic to several of the studio's films that became known as "the MGM look." Gibbons also designed the Academy Award statuette (later dubbed "Oscar") for the newly formed Academy of Motion Picture Arts and Sciences in 1927–28. With MGM architect Douglas Honnold, he built a modern home in Santa Monica in 1930 for himself and his first wife, actress Dolores Del Rio. JMM

Sources
- Christina Wilson, "Cedric Gibbons: Architect of Hollywood's Golden Age," in *Architecture and Film*, ed. Mark Lamster (New York: Princeton Architectural Press, 2000), 101–15.
- Michael Webb, "Cedric Gibbons and the MGM Style," *Architectural Digest* 47, no. 4 (April 1990): 100, 104, 108, 112.
- Lindy Jean Narver, "Cedric Gibbons: Pioneer in Art Direction for Cinema" (PhD diss., University of Southern California, 1988).

Gladding, McBean & Company (1875–1962), one of the "Big Five" California potteries (a group that also included J. A. Bauer Pottery Company, Metlox Manufacturing Company, Pacific Clay Products Company, and Vernon Kilns), was already a successful manufacturer of building materials, gardenware, and architectural terracotta when it ventured into the solid-color dinnerware market at the height of the Great Depression. Established in Lincoln, California, in 1875, by 1926 the company was the largest clay products manufacturer in the West, with plants in several locations in California and Washington State. In 1923 it acquired Tropico Potteries in Glendale, and by 1934 Frederic J. Grant was hired to manage a new department for the production of colorful tableware and artware. The trade name Franciscan Pottery was adopted to suggest a romantic association with California's Spanish past. The first dinnerware offering—the solid-color *El Patio* line, ultimately made in eighteen colors—was available from 1934 to 1953. The name was changed from Franciscan Pottery to Franciscan Ware in 1936, and these high-quality goods could be found in department stores across the United States. Hand-decorated patterns were introduced in 1937, the same year the company acquired Catalina Clay Products Company and manufactured several dinnerware and artware lines under the name Catalina Pottery. Franciscan unveiled fine china in 1942, followed by several new dinnerware lines in the years during and after World War II, including the wildly popular *Desert Rose* and *Starburst* patterns. Gladding, McBean merged with International Lock Joint and Pipe Company in 1962 to form Interpace. The new company hired Millard Sheets as design adviser, and he recruited ceramists Rupert Deese, Dora De Larios, Harrison McIntosh, Jerry Rothman, Henry Takemoto, and others to design architectural tile and dinnerware. Franciscan was purchased by Wedgwood in 1979, and the Glendale factory closed in 1984, with operations moving to England. JMM

Sources
- James F. Elliot-Bishop, *Franciscan, Catalina, and Other Gladding, McBean Wares* (Atglen, Pa.: Schiffer, 2001).

POTTERY ON PARADE...

Through all alert china departments marches a continuous stream of FRANCISCAN WARE — its outstanding success due to the exceptionally fine and durable body, perfect colorings and distinctive designs.

+ FRANCISCAN WARE +
REG. U.S. PAT. OFF.

GLADDING, McBEAN & CO....LOS ANGELES

Gladding, McBean & Company advertisement, 1936.

Glenn of California
1948–1992

Father and son Isaac and Robert Baron owned Arcadia-based Glenn of California, a manufacturer of furniture by such notable designers as Milo Baughman, Evans Clark, Greta Magnusson Grossman, John Kapel, Stewart MacDougall, and Kipp Stewart. When the Barons bought the furniture company Glenn Inc. in 1948, they changed the name to Glenn of California and retained some staff. The company name derived from the middle name of designer Stanley Glenn Young, who briefly remained at the company. Young and his colleague, salesman Harold Rose, had previously worked at Frank Brothers, the Long Beach emporium of contemporary furniture, thus establishing a link between the two modern design businesses that would continue for many years (not only did Frank Brothers retail Glenn furniture but Glenn also conducted photo shoots on the store's premises). The company produced furniture on a small-batch scale, making cuttings of about two hundred pieces at a time and employing a staff of 180 at its height. Most designs were made of solid wood or veneer, but Formica (Micarta), iron, and brass were also used. Glenn received national acclaim in 1952, when Greta Magnusson Grossman's side chair was included in MoMA's *Good Design* exhibition that year. The company's furniture was displayed in the *California Design* exhibitions and sold in modern shops such as Frank Brothers and Leslie's in Los Angeles, as well as through the Los Angeles and Chicago Furniture Marts. From the late 1960s until its closure in 1992, Glenn specialized in hotel and contract furniture. BT

Sources
· Study files, Balch Art Research Library, LACMA, DEC.002, including a company catalogue (c. 1952).

Glenn of California company catalogue, c. 1952. The Mr. and Mrs. Allan C. Balch Research Library, LACMA, Gift of Lloyd and Robert Baron.

Greta Magnusson Grossman
1906–1999

Born in Sweden, Greta Magnusson Grossman combined her Scandinavian design training with the relaxed lifestyle and furniture forms she admired in California to create livable modern interiors. Descended from a family of Swedish cabinetmakers, Grossman apprenticed as a woodworker in her hometown of Helsingborg before studying furniture, metalwork, and textiles at Konstfack, the art and design school in Stockholm. After a successful stint designing and manufacturing home furnishings in Sweden in the 1930s, Grossman and her Jewish British husband immigrated to the United States in 1940. The couple settled in Los Angeles, where she set up her own firm, offering custom interior design and furniture. Her architecture and interiors, characterized by the integration of modern furnishings with rustic materials and finishes, were regularly featured in leading design magazines such as *Arts and Architecture* and *Interiors*. In the early 1940s Grossman became associated with the downtown L.A. furniture emporium Barker Brothers, for which she created a line of furnishings and offered interior design services. In later years she designed for such companies as Glenn of California, Sherman Bertram Modern Color, and the lighting manufacturer Ralph O. Smith Company, and also screen-printed textiles. Her work gracefully brought together modern silhouettes and traditional materials, appealing to a clientele interested in casual, contemporary design. Her work appeared in several *California Design* exhibitions in the 1950s, and MoMA included her side chair made by Glenn of California in its 1952 *Good Design* exhibition. BT

Sources
· Evan Snyderman and Karin Åberg Wærn, eds., *Greta Magnusson Grossman—A Car and Some Shorts*, exh. cat. (Stockholm: Arkitekturmuseet, 2010).
· Evan Snyderman and Lily Kane, *Greta Magnusson Grossman, Designer*, exh. cat. (New York: R 20th Century Design, 2000).
· Rose Henderson, "A Swedish Furniture Designer in America," *American Artist*, December 1951, 54–57.

Victor Gruen
1903–1980

Called the "father of the shopping mall" for his invention of this ubiquitous architectural form, Austrian émigré Victor Gruen (né Gruenbaum) also designed exhibitions, stores, buildings, and entire urban plans. Gruen studied architecture at the Vienna Kunstakademi (Academy of Fine Arts) and considered Adolf Loos an influential teacher. Because of the depressed interwar economy, he focused on remodeling projects and became involved in socialist theater productions in the 1930s. When the Nazis annexed Austria in 1938, Gruen fled to New York City. There he worked on the 1939–40 World's Fair and develope a specialty in retail design. With Elsie Krummeck (see Elsie Crawford), he formed the firm Gruenbaum & Krummeck, and the pair moved to Los Angeles in 1941 to be closer to their important client, Grayson department store, marrying soon after. In 1950 he established Victor Gruen Associates with six partners—including Karl Van Leuven, Rudi Baumfeld, and Edgardo Contini—and opened offices in L.A. and around the country. Two projects contributed to his international reputation: Northland Center (1954), near Detroit, an early open-air shopping complex surrounded by a sea of parking, and Southdale Center (1956), near Minneapolis, the first enclosed shopping mall. Gruen envisioned building cities that would surround these cathedrals of consumption, comple with housing and municipal services that would resemble the urban neighborhoods of his native Vienna, but those plans were rarely realized. Gruen's firm was an incubator for young designers, with such employees as Carlos Diniz, Frank Gehry, Gere Kavanaugh, Marion Sampler, and Frederick A. Usher Jr. going on to establish successful independent careers. Late in life Gruen grew deeply troubled by the impact of his buildings and the proliferation of cars on the environment and social fabric. He spent the bulk of the 1960s and 1970s designing urban plans to resuscitate city centers. BT

Sources
- Victor Gruen Papers, Manuscript Division, Library of Congress, Washington, D.C.
- Alex Wall, *Victor Gruen: From Urban Shop to New City* (Barcelona: Actar, 2005).
- M. Jeffrey Hardwick, *Mall Maker: Victor Gruen, Architect of an American Dream* (Philadelphia: University of Pennsylvania Press, 2004).

Trude Guermonprez
1910–1976

Weaver and textile designer Trude Guermonprez received a progressive art education at Burg Giebichenstein (Municipal School of Fine and Applied Arts) in Halle, Germany, where she studied with weaver Benita Otte and sculptor Gerhard Marcks, both associated with the Bauhaus. In 1934 Guermonprez moved to the Netherlands and worked at the weaving studio Het Paapje. Forced into hiding during World War II, she immigrated to the United States in 1947 and was reunited with her family at Black Mountain College in North Carolina, where she taught weaving with Anni Albers. In 1949 Marguerite Wildenhain, a friend from Halle, invited Guermonprez to establish a weaving program at the Pond Farm Workshops, a school and community of craftspeople in Guerneville, in Northern California. After a brief tenure at Pond Farm, Guermonprez moved to CCAC in Oakland; she spent the remainder of her life as a weaving instructor there. An inspiring teacher, Guermonprez trained several students who went on to become influential in the field, including Carole Beadle, Lore Kadden Lindenfeld, and Kay Sekimachi. Guermonprez took on custom architectural commissions and designed for fashion and industrial textile manufacturers, including Owens-Corning Fiberglas and Du Pont Nylon Carpets. She is best known, however, for her role in the burgeoning fiber art movement. Her textile graphics (featuring figural images created by warp painting), space hangings (three-dimensional double-cloth structures), and word hangings (containing aphoristic messages executed in brocade) all expanded the boundaries of textile art. Guermonprez was an active member of the American Craft Council and the Designer-Craftsmen of California and received the Craftsmanship Medal from the American Institute of Architects (1970). Her tapestries were the subject of a posthumous exhibition at the Oakland Museum (1982). BT

Sources
- Dean and Geraldine Schwarz, eds., *Marguerite Wildenhain and the Bauhaus: An Eyewitness Anthology* (Decorah, Iowa: South Bear Press, 2007).
- Hazel V. Bray, *The Tapestries of Trude Guermonprez*, exh. cat. (Oakland: Oakland Museum, 1982).
- Dorothy Bryan, "Trude Guermonprez," *Handweaver & Craftsman*, Spring 1960, 30–31, 53–54.
- Yoshiko Uchida, "Trude Guermonprez," *Craft Horizons*, March/April 1959, 27–31.

Robert Guidi
1922–1977

Often employing whimsical sketches and portrait photographs in his work, graphic designer and art director Robert Guidi brought a bold yet playful style to his illustrations and layout designs. Born in Portland, Maine, he came to Los Angeles when his father, concert violinist Scipione Guidi, secured a job in Hollywood. While working for advertising agency Abbott Kimball, Guidi met Harry J. Pack, and, together with fellow employee and illustrator Bob McAvin, they founded Tri-Arts in 1949. After McAvin's departure about a year later, Guidi and Pack kept the name Tri-Arts, which stood for their work in the three fields of illustration, design, and production. The company employed about twenty people at its peak and was responsible for many print and television advertisements and album cover designs in the 1950s and 1960s. While Guidi's illustrations have a spontaneous, unstudied appearance, they were the result of a meticulous design process. Best known for his work with animator John Hubley and for his covers for Contemporary Records, Guidi often combined bold, hierarchical typefaces with a single photographic image; photographer William Claxton was a frequent collaborator. A member of the Art Directors Club of Los Angeles, Guidi received an award from the organization in 1953 and was frequently featured in its exhibitions of advertising art. JMM

Sources
- Amid Amidi, *Cartoon Modern: Style and Design in Fifties Animation* (San Francisco: Chronicle Books, 2006), 90–92.
- Study files, Balch Art Research Library, LACMA, DEC.002.

Contemporary C3509: Howard Rumsey's Lighthouse All-Stars * Barney Kessel * Hampton Hawes' Trio *with* Shelly Manne

LIGHTHOUSE AT LAGUNA

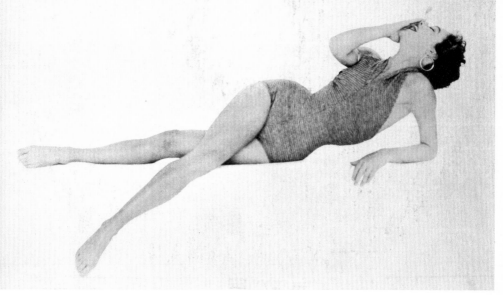

Robert Guidi, *Lighthouse at Laguna* (album cover), 1955.
LACMA, Decorative Arts and Design Council Fund.

Interior designer William Haines freely combined modern and historical sources to create glamorous settings for his celebrity and socialite clients. Born in Virginia, Haines moved to Los Angeles to pursue acting after winning the 1922 New Faces competition sponsored by the Goldwyn Picture Corp. (which later became part of MGM). The charismatic gay actor thrived in the relatively accepting climate of 1920s Hollywood, winning popular acclaim for his comedic talents. When MGM canceled his contract in 1933, he had already begun to establish himself as a decorator, designing a home for his friend and costar Joan Crawford in 1929 and opening an antiques shop with his former body double, Mitchell Foster, in 1930. Haines's client list grew quickly, and in 1935 Haines Foster Decorators opened a columned neoclassical studio on the Sunset Strip. In 1949, four years after Foster's retirement, the newly named firm, William Haines, Inc., relocated to the heart of Beverly Hills, where Haines designed an airy modern office that demonstrated his versatility as a decorator. His signature style combined ornate Asian antiques and dramatic period details with sleek modern touches, such as Lucite fixtures and built-in furniture. He created custom furniture and lighting for his clients, working with staff designers Michael Morrison, Paul Féher, and associate Ted Graber, who continued the firm after Haines's death. Haines advocated collaboration between architects, interior designers, and landscape designers, as exemplified by his interiors for the Brody House (1950), designed by A. Quincy Jones with landscaping by Garrett Eckbo. He tailored his aesthetic to each project, demonstrating equal comfort with furnishing the open spaces of Jones's modern architecture and with creating elaborate, period-inspired interiors. His last major commission was the renovation of Winfield House (1969), the official London residence of U.S. ambassador Walter Annenberg. ss

Sources
- William Haines Archives, the Huntington Library, Art Collections, and Botanical Gardens, San Marino, California.
- Peter Schifando and Jean H. Mathison, *Class Act: William Haines, Legendary Hollywood Decorator* (New York: Pointed Leaf Press, 2005).

Hawk House
1950s

Home accessories manufacturer Hawk House produced affordable metal housewares in the 1950s. Stan Hawk Jr. (1904–1958) and his wife, Ethyle Hawk (1903–1987), operated the small firm from their Harwell Hamilton Harris–designed home in Silver Lake. Their products, which included lamps, ashtrays, and several variations on a barbecue-brazier, were sold at modern design shops such as the Pacific Shop in San Francisco and Carroll Sagar & Associates in Los Angeles. The simple but versatile iron barbecue-brazier attributed to R. Coelho-Cordoza—which could be used both indoors and outdoors and could also function as a coffee table, wine cooler, or planter—garnered national recognition, appearing in the first *California Design* exhibition (1954–55) and in the Albright Art Gallery's traveling exhibition *20th Century Design: U.S.A.* (1958–59), as well as in several design publications. ss

Sources
· Study files, Balch Art Research Library, LACMA, DEC.002.

R. Coelho-Cordoza (attributed) for Hawk House, Barbecue-brazier, c. 1948.

Heath Ceramics
founded 1946

Sausalito pottery manufacturer Heath Ceramics is renowned for architectural tile and durable, well-constructed tablewares made using small-batch production methods. Its founder, Edith Heath (1911–2005), was introduced to ceramics at Chicago Teachers College (graduated 1934) and studied part-time at the Art Institute of Chicago (1934–39). Edith met and married Brian Heath (1913–2001) in 1938, and in 1941 the couple moved to San Francisco. Edith converted their basement laundry room into her first ceramic studio, took extension courses in ceramic chemistry at the University of California, Berkeley, and developed a distinctive clay body from local materials. Her first show, at the California Palace of the Legion of Honor (1944), led to a retail arrangement with Gump's department store, which provided her with a small workshop. The business grew rapidly: Brian became Edith's business partner, and a handful of employees helped produce the wheel-thrown goods. When distributor N. S. Gustin Company offered to represent Heath Ceramics nationwide in 1946, the Heaths rented factory space in Sausalito and shifted from duplicate production by hand to a semiautomated process using a pug mill and jiggering wheel. Applying Edith's skills as a studio potter to design for production, the firm unveiled *Coupe*, its first dinnerware line, in 1947. By late 1960 it had moved operations to a new factory in Sausalito and introduced the *Rim* line. With the help of French ceramist Leon Galleto, who had joined Heath in 1958, and a machine devised by Brian, the company expanded into architectural tile production. In addition to its standard production lines, Heath received several special commissions. Notable projects included tile installations at LACMA and the Pasadena Art Museum and a custom dinnerware line for the gourmet Berkeley restaurant Chez Panisse. Heath Ceramics was exhibited widely, including at the inaugural *Good Design* exhibition at MoMA (1950). JMM

Sources
· Mija Riedel, "Building Bridges," *American Craft* 68, no. 1 (February/March 2008): 104–12.
· Amos Klausner, ed., *Heath Ceramics: The Complexity of Simplicity* (San Francisco: Chronicle Books, 2006).
· Edith Heath, "Tableware and Tile for the World, Heath Ceramics, 1944–1994," interview by Rosalie Ross, 1990–1992, 1994, Regional Oral History Office, Bancroft Library, University of California, Berkeley.
· Heath Ceramics (website), www.heathceramics.com.

Edith Heath with company wares, 1950s.

Otto Heino
1915–2009
Vivika Heino
1910–1995

Prolific studio potters and educators known for their vessel forms and innovative glazes, Otto and Vivika Heino were influential fixtures in the postwar craft community. Born Vivien Place in Caledonia, New York, Vivika first came to California in 1934. She studied and worked in various craft fields in Los Angeles and Carmel before settling in San Francisco, where she took night classes in ceramics and discovered her artistic calling. She worked as an assistant to Glen Lukens at USC from 1940 to 1942 until Professor Charles Harder invited her to New York to study ceramics at Alfred University (MFA, 1944). Otto was born Aho Heino in East Hampton, Connecticut, and became interested in ceramics after visiting potteries while stationed in England during World War II; he observed the renowned potter Bernard Leach and resolved to learn the craft after the war. In 1948 Otto enrolled in a class that Vivika was teaching at the League of New Hampshire Arts and Crafts, and the couple married two years later. They moved west in 1952 so Vivika could teach at USC while Lukens was on sabbatical. The couple originally intended to stay for a year but remained in L.A. until 1963. Vivika, a respected and influential educator, taught at USC from 1952 to 1955 and at Chouinard Art Institute from 1955 to 1963; Otto also taught at those institutions while working as a potter. During this time the Heinos opened The Pottery, the first shop in L.A. that sold strictly handmade pots. In 1963 Vivika accepted a position at the Rhode Island School of Design, and two years later the Heinos returned to New Hampshire. In 1973 they moved back to California and established their workshop and gallery in Ojai in the former home of Beatrice Wood. Their pots have been featured in hundreds of exhibitions and are held in museum collections worldwide. JMM

Sources
· Kevin V. Wallace and Tim Schiffer, *The Art of Vivika and Otto Heino*, exh. cat. (Ventura, Calif.: Ventura County Museum of History & Art, 2005).
· Margaret Carney, Val Cushing, and Gerry Williams, *What You Give Away You Keep Forever: The Vivika and Otto Heino Retrospective*, exh. cat. (Alfred: Museum of Ceramic Art, New York State College of Ceramics at Alfred University, 1995).
· Otto and Vivika Heino, interview by Elaine Levin, March 4, 1981, Archives of American Art, Smithsonian Institution.

Tony Hill
1908–1975

A prominent member of Los Angeles's African American artistic circle, ceramist Tony Hill served as a mentor and role model when few opportunities existed for black artists. He sold his line of functional handmade lamps, ashtrays, and bowls at prominent shops and showrooms throughout the United States and internationally, including at Marshall Field's in Chicago. In his work he contrasted thick, creamy glazes with a textured stoneware clay to create forms that suited a variety of interiors, often matching custom colors to his clients' homes. William Anthony Hill III was born in St. Joseph, Missouri, and studied at the University of Kansas, furthering his education with graduate courses in social work at the University of Chicago. He was a social worker in Chicago and briefly in New York City until 1942, when he relocated to Los Angeles seeking opportunities for his wife, actress Frances Williams. Unsatisfied with a job in an aircraft factory, he pursued an earlier interest in pottery, enrolling in night classes at USC with Glen Lukens. Lukens encouraged Hill and fellow artist Wilmer James to open their own studio, and in 1944 they founded the Ceramics Workshop on Jefferson Boulevard in South Central Los Angeles. The partnership dissolved after several years, but as the demand for his accessories increased, Hill hired assistants to keep up with the orders. In 1974 Hill celebrated his thirtieth year in business by organizing the Art-Fair Gallery, a three-month venture that showcased his studio along with work by local artists. Hill forged strong personal connections in the community and guided several younger artists—including John Outterbridge and Dale Brockman Davis—through the complex local networks of artists and patrons. ss

Sources
- "Tony Hill in 30th Year at Community Art Fair," *Los Angeles Sentinel*, October 17, 1974.
- "On a Talent That's Kneaded: Tony Hill, Ceramist and His Work," *Designs*, January 1948, 25–26.
- "Ceramics by Tony Hill," *Ebony*, November 1946, 31–35.
- Study files, Balch Art Research Library, LACMA, DEC.002.

J. A. Bauer Pottery Company
1885–1962

When J. A. Bauer Pottery Company penetrated the national tableware market in around 1930 with its *Ringware* line, the American public saw that a beautiful table could be set using vibrantly colored pottery inspired by the Southern California landscape and a palette associated with Mexico. Founder J. Andy Bauer (1856–1923) opened his first factory in 1885 in Paducah, Kentucky, and then moved the business to the Lincoln Heights neighborhood of Los Angeles around 1910. The company introduced dinnerware under the direction of Danish-born designer and mold maker Louis Ipsen, who had been hired by the pottery in about 1916, and its signature bright glazes were devised by ceramics engineer Victor Houser, hired in the late 1920s. In 1935 Bauer purchased the nearby facility of bankrupt tile manufacturer Batchelder-Wilson, allowing for the dramatic expansion and introduction of new designs, clay bodies, and glaze colors. Bauer, which was a member of the group known as the "Big Five" (see Gladding, McBean & Company), formed the California Pottery Guild in 1937 to promote their brightly colored wares on a national scale, capitalizing on the marketability of "California" and competing with manufacturers in other regions who had begun introducing solid-color designs (most notably the *Fiesta* line, introduced in 1936 by Homer Laughlin China Company in West Virginia). Bauer produced hotel-grade china cereal bowls and poultry feeders under defense contracts during World War II and resumed dinnerware production after the war. Owing to increased competition from other manufacturers, plastic alternatives, low-cost Japanese imports, and labor unrest, the company ceased operations in 1962. JMM

Sources
- Jack Chipman, *Collector's Encyclopedia of Bauer Pottery* (Paducah, Ky.: Collector Books, 1999).
- Mitch Tuchman, *Bauer: Classic American Pottery* (San Francisco: Chronicle Books, 1995).

J. A. Bauer Pottery Company catalogue, 1939. Courtesy of the Museum of California Design.

Furniture designer Dan Johnson brought a sculptural sensibility to his work, including his most recognized design, the graceful, animal-like *Gazelle* chair (1959). Born in Missouri, Johnson moved to Los Angeles in 1940 to attend Art Center School on a work-study scholarship. He briefly studied at the University of Cincinnati Engineering College before returning to Art Center in 1945. In the late 1940s Johnson designed a full line of wood furniture for Alhambra-based manufacturer Hayden Hall. Many of the pieces from this line were photographed in Case Study House #17 by Rodney Walker and published in *Arts and Architecture* magazine. In the early 1950s Johnson designed several chairs, many with tubular steel frames and flexible seating surfaces of cord or reed. Later that decade he moved to Italy, where he launched Dan Johnson Studio in Rome and developed the *Gazelle* line of tables, chairs, and sculptures in walnut, bronze, and gold-anodized aluminum, describing them as "a modern approach to the ancient Roman stuff I appreciated so much in Italy."[1] The *Gazelle* line was not a commercial success; according to Johnson's records, only about 150 pieces were made and imported to the United States, and sales were dismal. The initial distributor, Arch Industries, ceased to carry the line in 1959 because of slow sales and costs to repair damage incurred during shipping, and an indebted Johnson struggled to find a new distributor. Johnson's work was included in several *California Design* exhibitions, and he also worked as an architect. JMM

1.
Dan Johnson to Ethel, George, Mike, and Chris,
January 28, 1961, Dan Johnson Archive.

Sources
· Dan Johnson Archive, Chicago. Privately held.
· Study files, Balch Art Research Library, LACMA,
DEC.002.

DeDe Johnson
c. 1912–n.d.

Fashion designer DeDe Johnson created stylish sportswear suited to casual California living and is credited as the originator of the modern pedal pusher. Many details of Johnson's life are difficult to confirm; she was reportedly thirty-three years old in 1946 when she took a well-publicized tumble from the rim of the Grand Canyon during a fashion event (she recovered quickly from her injuries). Johnson started out as a model for Corinne Costuming Company in Hollywood, later appearing in New York shows and traveling the country modeling for manufacturers. She began designing in the 1930s and worked for a dress firm before launching her own business, DeDe Johnson Sportswear, in Los Angeles in the early 1940s. Around this time she married Harold Kronthal, a fabric converter who also served as her business manager. Johnson quickly made a name for herself with wearable fashions that were both inventive and well tailored. Feminine and suited to an active lifestyle, her designs helped popularize California sportswear throughout the country. Her 1944 pedal-pusher ensemble was the first of a number of fashion innovations, which included "Cloud Stroller" culottes (1946), a sleeveless jacket (1949), and the band-top skirt (1960). Johnson was honored as a living legend of California fashion by the Los Angeles Fashion Group in 1976. JMM

Sources
- Virginia Scallon, "California Sportswear Designer Climbs Success Ladder Quickly," *Christian Science Monitor*, March 28, 1945.
- Study files, Balch Art Research Library, LACMA, DEC.002.

De De Johnson

COHAMA

HAND-SCREENED IN CALIFORNIA

Advertisement for Cohama featuring DeDe Johnson design, 1947.

John Kapel
b. 1922

Furniture maker John Kapel worked as both a designer and a craftsman, making models for furniture companies to produce and unique pieces in his studio for private clients, the latter a practice he continues today. Born in Cleveland, Kapel studied briefly with industrial designer Viktor Schreckengost at the Cleveland Institute of Art and served in the U.S. Navy during World War II. In 1947–48 he studied architecture and design at Charles University in Prague, returning to the United States after the Soviet-backed Czech coup. At Schreckengost's suggestion, Kapel enrolled at the Cranbrook Academy of Art to study industrial design (MA, 1951). After graduation, he worked in New York City for Swedish Modern, an importer of Swedish furniture, and subsequently in the office of industrial designer George Nelson. From both jobs he gained insight into the business of furniture production. Inspired by an article about the work and lifestyle of Sam Maloof, who was making furniture at his rural home in Alta Loma, Kapel decided to change coasts and careers. Disliking Los Angeles and finding the weather in San Diego too pleasant to be productive, he first settled in Saratoga, outside San Jose. In 1960 he designed his home and studio in Woodside, handcrafting all of the interior finishes himself. He designed solid wood and veneered furniture for production by several companies, including Glenn of California, Kosuga, and Gall Furniture, alongside his custom work. His furniture reflected Scandinavian idioms of organic shapes and exquisitely carved forms and often employed fine exotic woods. In both his production and handmade furniture, he displayed an equal concern for functionality and aesthetics. He has also worked as a sculptor and jewelry designer. BT

Sources
- Glenn Adamson, "California Dreaming," in *Furniture Studio: Heart of the Functional Arts* (Free Union, Va.: Furniture Society, 1999), 32–43.
- Priscilla Ginsberg, "A Cabinet Maker's Dream House," *Interiors*, November 1961, 132–45.
- Study files, Balch Art Research Library, LACMA, DEC.002.

Gere Kavanaugh
b. 1929

A versatile designer whose work ranges from toys and graphics to entire interior scheme Gere Kavanaugh has been an important member of the Los Angeles design community since the early 1960s. She draws inspiration from folk and vernacular art, frequently incorporating a vibrant color palette and sense of play in her work, and is a vocal advoca for unhindered creative expression. Born in Tennessee, she graduated from the Memphis Academy of Art (BA, 1951) and later attended the Cranbrook Academy of Art (MA, 1953 where she studied with architect and designer Theodore Luderowski, ceramist Maija Grotell, and weaver Marianne Strengell. Upon graduation, Kavanaugh worked for Genera Motors as a designer in the company's architecture department before accepting a position at Victor Gruen Associates (see Victor Gruen) in Los Angeles in 1960. At Gruen she was responsible for coordinated interiors, including textiles, lighting, furniture, and graphics. A regular client was Joseph Magnin, the San Francisco–based specialty fashion retailer, for which she designed several distinctive shop interiors. In 1964 Kavanaugh established her own firm, Gere Kavanaugh/Designs, where her long client list included Hallmark Greeting Cards, the Irish Board of Trade, and Isabel Scott Fabrics. Another maj aspect of her work has been exhibition design for such institutions as the Craft and Folk Art Museum in Los Angeles, where she also cocurated the show *Home Sweet Home: American Domestic Vernacular Architecture* (1983). She received the International Design Award from the American Institute of Interior Designers in 1968 for her textile design, and her work was featured in several *California Design* exhibitions beginning in 1961. LS

Sources
· Ella Howard, "The Design 'Adventure' of Gere Kavanaugh," *Studies in the Decorative Arts* 8, no. 1 (Fall/Winter 2000–2001): 153–60.
· Sharon E. Fay, "Designer Lets All Her Talent Go to Work," *Los Angeles Times*, March 20, 1969.
· Jim Morgan, "The Work of Gere Kavanaugh: Profile of a Designer," *Interiors* 134 (January 1957): 70–71, 74–75.
· Study files, Balch Art Research Library, LACMA, DEC.002.

Henry C. Keck
b. 1921

Henry C. Keck designed some of the twentieth century's most ubiquitous commercial products that have remained in production for decades: the flashing roadside barricade lights that alert drivers to hazards up ahead; the iconic slanted-top salt, pepper, and sugar shakers found in diners across the country; and the automatic Bobrick hand dryers affixed to the walls of many public restrooms. Born in New York City, Keck was raised in New Jersey in a family of prominent artists, most notably his father, sculptor Maxfield Keck, and his uncles, sculptor Charles Keck and stained-glass artist Henry Keck. The younger Keck studied business and engineering at Dartmouth (BA, 1943) and worked briefly at Lockheed before volunteering for the U.S. Navy. He finished his training in electronics at the Naval Research Laboratories in Washington, D.C., and subsequently studied industrial design at the California Institute of Technology in Pasadena (MA, 1947). After graduation, he worked for Corning Glass Works in New York State before returning to Southern California to work as assistant manager in designer Raymond Loewy's Los Angeles office. He founded the industrial design firm Keck-Craig with engineer Burnie Craig (1911–2003) in 1951, remaining there until 2006, when he retired to become a consultant. Though small, Keck-Craig attracted prominent clients such as Shell Chemical, Union Carbide, and Avery Products (now Avery Dennison). The firm won recognition for its efficient engineering and manufacturing solutions as well as its minimalist designs. Though not as well known as more celebrated figures in the design world—Henry Dreyfuss was his friend and neighbor—Keck showed work in nearly every *California Design* exhibition and in many international design publications. ss

Sources
· Henry C. Keck, *How Design Changed America: Crossing the Great Divide between Art and Engineering: An Historical Memoir* (self-published, 2010).
· Karen Kaplan, "A Classic Realm of Design," *Los Angeles Times*, January 1, 2001.
· Study files, Balch Art Research Library, LACMA, DEC.002.

Henry C. Keck (right) and Burnie Craig.

Corita Kent, also known as Sister Corita, was born Frances Kent in Fort Dodge, Iowa, and raised in Los Angeles. A celebrated figure in the L.A. art community, she brought an unconventional approach and contagious enthusiasm to teaching and printmaking that galvanized her students and contemporaries. Kent took the name Sister Mary Corita upon entering the Order of the Immaculate Heart of Mary in 1936. After graduating from L.A.'s Immaculate Heart College (IHC) in 1941, she returned there to teach art in 1946. She continued her education at USC, experimenting with screenprinting in her final semester (MA, 1951). An early print, *the lord is with thee*, received first prize in a 1952 exhibition at the Los Angeles Museum of History, Science and Art (now LACMA) and at the California State Fair in the print division. This recognition encouraged her to continue exploring the medium, and she began to use her art as a form of critique, taking aim at such varied targets as the Vietnam War, conservative elements in the Catholic Church, and rampant consumerism. Kent was a committed social activist, and her imagery, often drawn from the vernacular urban environment, treated words as images and used wide-ranging cultural references, from quotations by Gandhi to advertising slogans. She led the progressive art program at IHC from 1964 to 1968, but her work extended far beyond the college community through public events such as the annual Mary's Day celebrations. Among the many notable figures in her circle, she credited Charles Eames, Buckminster Fuller, and art historian Dr. Alois Schardt for their important roles in her intellectual and artistic growth. Sister Corita formally resigned from the order in 1968 and lived and worked in Boston as Corita Kent. The U.S. Postal Authority published her "Love" stamp one year before her death. JMM

Sources
- Corita Papers, 1936–1992, Schlesinger Library, Radcliffe Institute, Harvard University, Cambridge, Massachusetts.
- Julie Ault, *Come Alive! The Spirited Art of Sister Corita* (London: Four Corners Books, 2006).
- "Los Angeles Art Community: Group Portrait, Corita Kent," interview by Bernard Galm, 1977, Oral History Program, University of California, Los Angeles.
- Corita Art Center (website), www.corita.org.

Bernard Kester
b. 1928

A textile designer and ceramist, Bernard Kester also has been an eloquent critic of California craft in his many roles as teacher, writer, exhibition designer, and curator. Kester studied art at UCLA (BA, 1950; MA, 1955). Equally proficient in his two chosen fields, he created vivid patterns for furnishing textiles and expertly threw and glazed elegant ceramic vessels. As a professor of art at UCLA from 1956 to 1993, he taught design, ceramics, and weaving. In addition to his teaching responsibilities, he took on a dizzying number of extracurricular activities to promote individual craftspeople and advance the state of the field. He was a frequent correspondent on developments in the California craft scene for *Craft Horizons* magazine, an active member of the American Craft Council, a trustee of the American Craft Museum in New York, and a board member of the Craft and Folk Art Museum in Los Angeles. Kester's ceramics and hand-printed textiles have been featured in dozens of exhibitions, and he displayed work in every *California Design* show, as well as being responsible for the overall exhibition design of the 1968, 1971, and 1976 installations. As a curator, he organized several groundbreaking exhibitions on contemporary craft and fiber art, most notably *Deliberate Entanglements* at UCLA (1971), and he designed dozens of exhibitions and installations at LACMA between 1966 and 2011. BT

Sources
· Beverly Johnson, "The Artistry in Hand-Printed Fabrics," *Los Angeles Times*, February 5, 1967.
· Study files, Balch Art Research Library, LACMA, DEC.002.

Albert Henry King
1900–1982
Louisa Etcheverry King
1911–1966

Colorist and teacher Albert Henry King was among the earliest Southern California ceramists to work in porcelain. Together, he and his wife, Louisa Etcheverry King, created Asian-inspired ceramic wares and prominent public mosaic murals. Born in England, Albert King came to Los Angeles with his family in 1911. He studied at the Cannon School of Art before embarking on a commercial art career. He worked in both ceramic design and film, producing special effects for films such as Cecil B. DeMille's *The Ten Commandments* (1923). He began regularly attending the Art Students League of Los Angeles in 1923, studying color and composition with painter Stanton Macdonald-Wright. There he met fellow student Louisa Etcheverry, a Los Angeles native whose family ran a commercial pottery in Vernon. In the 1930s the couple, who later married, collaborated on projects for the Works Progress Administration (WPA), where Albert headed the ceramic and mosaic department. Louisa succeeded him in this role when he became WPA district supervisor for Southern California in 1938. Of their many projects for the WPA, most significant was a massive ceramic mosaic for the Long Beach Municipal Auditorium (1937), which Albert codesigned with Macdonald-Wright and Henry Allen Nord. In 1931 King and partner Harold Spence established what became the Lotus & Acanthus Studio in Los Angeles and built a kiln that allowed them to fire porcelain, a material that had long been the domain of commercial producers because of its high-firing requirements. They produced limited-production cast vessels influenced by Asian ceramics as well as figurines sculpted by Etcheverry, who managed operations after Spence's departure in 1936. Over time their production increasingly emphasized unique works as Albert began to throw bowls, vases, and bottles and developed vivid glazes inspired by Chinese ceramics. His interest in color and optics carried across many media. As a founding member of the Art Center School faculty in 1931, he taught courses on all aspects of color until the late 1960s and later lent his expertise as a color consultant to clients such as the Rand Corporation and Eastman Kodak. ss

Sources
- Albert Henry King Papers, 1913–1963, Archives of American Art, Smithsonian Institution.
- Art Center College of Design Archives, Pasadena.
- Will South, Marian Toshiki-Kovinick, and Julia Armstrong-Totten, *A Seed of Modernism: The Art Students League of Los Angeles, 1906–1953* (Pasadena: Pasadena Museum of California Art; Berkeley: Heyday Books, 2008).

Maria Kipp
1900–1988

Textile designer and weaver Maria Kipp created distinctive handwoven fabrics through her firm Maria Kipp, Inc., the foremost producer of custom textiles in Los Angeles at mid-century. A native of Bavaria, Germany, she attended the Kunstgewerbeschule (School of Applied Arts) in Munich from 1918 to 1920 and was the first woman to enroll at Staatliche Hohere Fachschule für Textilindustrie (State Academy for the Textile Industry) in Münchberg. After graduating as a textile engineer in 1923, she began her weaving career. In 1924 Kipp moved to Los Angeles with her first husband, Ernst Haeckel, and they established Maria Haeckel Handweaves. Following their divorce in 1931, Kipp opened her own firm under her birth name. Renowned for her custom weaves for the many architects, decorators, designers, and agents who were her clients—R. M. Schindler, Richard Neutra, Paul T. Frankl, and Greta Magnusson Grossman among them—Kipp incorporated unusual textures and materials such as Lurex and metallic threads and used an extensive, often subtle, color palette for fabrics that were both attractive and utilitarian. Kipp's delicate handweaves complemented the open, sun-drenched spaces of modern California interiors and mitigated the intense light that poured in through large windows. She designed each textile on the loom and worked out the details of each commission before turning it over to her weavers. Maria Kipp, Inc., managed by her second husband, George Engelke, thrived in the postwar period, employing a staff of twenty-eight in 1956 and producing designs for hotels, department stores, public buildings, and private homes. Kipp retired in 1977, but Maria Kipp, Inc., continued to operate until 1996. JMM

Sources
· Kipp Collection, Western Textile Center, San Bernardino County Museum, California.
· Maria Kipp, autobiography written for family, 1977–79, Dorothy Stein Research Center for Costume and Textiles, LACMA.
· Anne Lawrence, "Feminist Design Methodology: Considering the Case of Maria Kipp" (master's thesis, University of North Texas, 2003).
· Marlyn R. Musicant, "Maria Kipp: Autobiography of a Hand Weaver," *Studies in the Decorative Arts* 8, no. 1 (Fall/Winter 2000–2001): 92–107.
· Dorothy Bryan, "Maria Kipp—Her Career as a Weaver," *Handweaver and Craftsman* 3, no. 1 (Winter 1951–52): 15–17, 59.

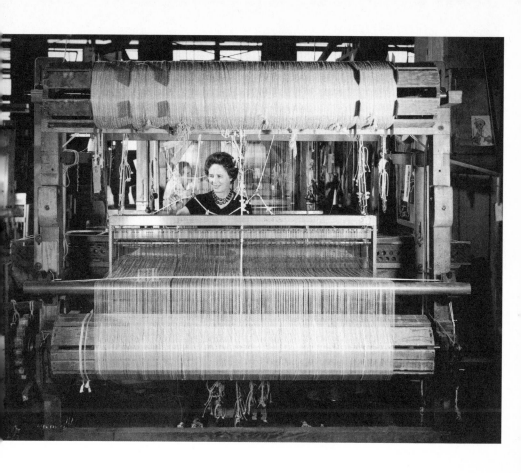

Charles Kratka
1922–2007

A native Southern Californian, Charles Kratka studied art at UCLA and graduated from the advertising design department at Art Center School in 1948, where Alvin Lustig was an influential instructor and mentor. In 1947 he began working as a graphic designer for Charles and Ray Eames, creating advertisements and catalogues for the Herman Miller Furniture Company, the manufacturer of Eames furniture. Since the Eames Office was small at that time, Kratka was involved in many other capacities as well, including furniture and exhibition design. From the late 1940s to the mid-1950s he freelanced, creating covers and interior layouts for *Arts and Architecture* magazine and teaching advertising design at Art Center School. Later in his career Kratka shifted his emphasis to interiors, becoming head of interior design at the architectural firm Pereira & Luckman in 1957. In this role he was responsible for several large projects, including the colorful abstract mosaics located in the tunnels connecting the terminals to the street at Los Angeles International Airport (1961), and the interiors of LACMA, which opened in Hancock Park in 1965. In 1967 he established his own firm, Charles Kratka Interior Planning and Design, and completed several large commissions, including the expansion of the Times Mirror Company building in downtown L.A. (1973). BT

Sources
- Valerie J. Nelson, "Charles D. Kratka, 85; Designer, Artist Created Mosaic Tunnel Walls at LAX," *Los Angeles Times*, November 25, 2007.
- Study files, Balch Art Research Library, LACMA, DEC.002.

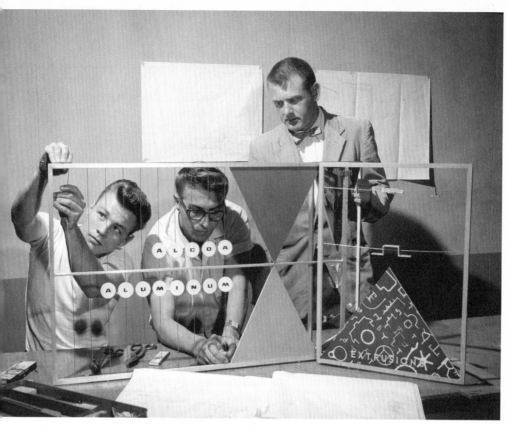

Charles Kratka (right) with Art Center School students, c. 1955.

Architect and designer Walter Lamb was renowned for his elegant outdoor furniture made of patinated metal tubing and hand-wrapped cord. Originally from Wichita, Kansas, Lamb was raised in San Francisco and studied architecture at the University of California Berkeley, before moving to Honolulu in 1922. There he worked on commissions for private homes and commercial buildings, the most significant being the interiors and furniture for the Royal Hawaiian Hotel in Waikiki. The idea for his highly acclaimed patio and poolside furniture originated during World War II, and it has been claimed that the early hand-wrought furnishings were made of bronze from ships sunk in Pearl Harbor and strung with reclaimed cotton yacht cord. Curvilinear and reductive in form, Lamb's patio furniture is a translation of the tubular steel designs of European modernism into forms suitable for California's culture of indoor/outdoor living. Returning to San Francisco after the war, Lamb sold the patents for his lounge designs to Pasadena-based Brown Jordan Company, which produced the furniture until the 1970s and then reprised it in 2009. Praised in home decor magazines for its practicality and durability, the Lamb line was touted for its use of bronze, which, unlike iron, did not rust (though recent scientific testing has revealed that the metal alloy is actually brass). Lamb's *Waikiki* lounge was included in the *Good Design* exhibition at MoMA (1952), and his work appeared in the first *California Design* exhibition (1954–55). Later in his life, Lamb lived and worked in Pebble Beach and Montecito, California. LS

Sources
· Lily Kane, "Champions of Leisure: Outdoor Furniture from California," *Modernism* 5, no. 2 (Summer 2002): 48–55.
· Study files, Balch Art Research Library, LACMA, DEC.002.

Walter Lamb for Brown Jordan Company, Chaise, c. 1954.
LACMA, Gift of Joel and Margaret Chen of J. F. Chen.

Walter Landor
1913–1995

Walter Landor was a pioneer in the field of corporate identity design, defining the graphic program and public image of dozens of internationally recognized brands. Born Walter Landauer in Munich, Landor moved to London in 1931 to study at Goldsmiths College of Art. In 1935 he joined designers Milner Gray and Misha Black to form Industrial Design Partnership, one of Britain's first consultant industrial design firms. Landor traveled to New York City in 1939, ostensibly to assist with and report on the World's Fair for British publications, but most likely he was looking to settle in the United States. After touring several cities, he chose San Francisco, where he founded his firm Walter Landor and Associates in 1941 with his wife, designer Josephine (Jo) Martinelli Landor (1918–2001). The firm took on projects ranging from environmental signage to retail interiors to product design but won the greatest acclaim for its packaging and identity schemes for such prominent corporate clients as Kellogg's (1960), General Electric (1986–88), and several major airlines. A champion of marketing research, Landor emphasized a humanistic approach that encouraged consumers to relate to mass-produced goods, using vernacular lettering styles for such classic designs as the logos for Del Monte Foods (c. 1967) and Levi Strauss & Co. (c. 1968). To brand his own company as a daring, creative enterprise, he moved his offices to the *Klamath*, a decommissioned wooden ferryboat docked in San Francisco Bay in 1964; the firm remained there until the mid-1980s. After building the business and establishing several international offices, Landor sold the firm to advertising giant Young & Rubicam and retired in 1989. ss

Sources
· Landor Design Collection, c. 1930–1994, Archives Center, National Museum of American History, Smithsonian Institution.
· Bernard F. Gallagher, "A Brand Is Built in the Mind: Walter Landor and the Transformation of Industrial Design in the Twentieth Century" (master's thesis, Cooperstown Graduate Program, State University of New York College at Oneonta, 2007).
· Ken Kelley and Rick Clogher, "The Ultimate Image Maker," *San Francisco Focus*, August 1992, 64–67, 114–19.

Walter Landor (center) and his staff with design studies for
Old Fitzgerald whiskey, c. 1960.

Doyle Lane
1925–2002

A studio ceramist and artist whose work ranged from large-scale murals to clay vessels with tactile surfaces evocative of nature, Doyle Lane succeeded in making a living from his craft—a notable achievement for any craftsperson, particularly an African American working at mid-century. By the early 1950s the Louisiana native had settled in Los Angeles and was working as a glaze technician for L. H. Butcher Company, a chemical supplier. He studied ceramics at Los Angeles City College (AA, 1953) before attending USC, probably taking courses with F. Carlton Ball. In his studio in the El Sereno district of East Los Angeles, Lane made functional earthenware and stoneware pots and experimented widely with glazes. During the 1960s he created murals and mosaics for architectural commissions. He also made clay paintings, applying glaze to clay slabs fired under high temperatures that resulted in vivid color combinations and textured surfaces. Later in his career Lane made ceramic beads and jewelry. His work was shown in several *California Design* exhibitions as well as in the traveling exhibition *Objects: USA* (1969) and *California Black Craftsmen* (Mills College Art Gallery, 1970). Like other African American artists, he found few galleries willing to exhibit his work and would later credit the Brockman Gallery in Leimert Park and the Ankrum Gallery on La Cienega Boulevard for helping to establish his reputation as an artist. JMM

Sources
· Thomas Riggs, ed., *St. James Guide to Black Artists* (Detroit: St. James Press, 1997), 313–14.
· Samella Lewis, *African American Art and Artists*, (Berkeley: University of California Press, 1990), 228.
· Stanley Wilson, "Black Artists of Los Angeles," *Studio Potter* 9, no. 2 (June 1981): 16–25.
· Study files, Balch Art Research Library, LACMA, DEC.002.

Marget Larsen
1922–1984

Marget Larsen designed advertising, packaging, and signage characterized by vivid color and bold typography, creating strikingly contemporary work that often incorporated historical motifs. A lifelong Bay Area resident, Larsen had some formal art education and studied with Margaret De Patta and Surrealist sculptor Robert Boardman Howard. In the 1950s and early 1960s she was art director for the San Francisco specialty-store chain Joseph Magnin, a rare position for a woman at the time. With her colleagues, fashion illustrator Betty Brader and advertising manager Toni Harley, she developed the store's image through advertisements and collectible gift boxes. Using intense colors, layered contemporary patterns, and stylized illustrations, they reinforced the store's appeal to a youthful, fashion-conscious audience. In 1964 Larsen became a freelance designer, often collaborating with her longtime partner, Robert Brewster Freeman (1908–1992). Together they founded Intrinsics, Inc., a small design branch of Freeman's advertising business that developed paper products ranging from colorful lunch boxes to a functional cardboard interpretation of the bentwood Thonet chair. Her advertising work reflected the same irreverence, bucking industry preferences for large images and logos in favor of text-based campaigns whose intricate designs recalled newspaper layouts. These advertisements, designed with copywriter Howard Gossage, defined the straightforward, intellectual aesthetic of organizations like the Sierra Club, and became *New Yorker* staples. By contrast, her packaging and signage incorporated splashes of pattern and color and stenciled lettering, best exemplified by her supergraphics for Shandygaff restaurant in San Francisco (1971) and her packages for Parisian Bakeries (1961), purveyors of San Francisco's famous sourdough bread. Larsen's work was frequently featured in *Communication Arts*, among other design publications. ss

Sources
- Robert Brewster Freeman, "Marget Larsen," *Communication Arts*, March/April 1988, 87–102.
- Barbara J. Allen, "Intrinsics," *Industrial Design*, June 1967, 36–37.

Paul László
1900–1993

Dubbed the "rich man's architect" by *Time* magazine in August 1952, Hungarian-born and Beverly Hills–based designer Paul László created lavish interior designs that catered to his clients' desire for luxury and comfort. László studied architecture and interior decoration at Staatliche Akademie der Bildenden Künste Stuttgart (Stuttgart State Academy of Art and Design) and established his own firm in Vienna in 1924, which he moved to Stuttgart in 1927. After the Nazis rose to power, László, one of whose grandparents was Jewish, immigrated to Los Angeles in 1936. During his long career as a furniture and interior designer, he built a diverse clientele ranging from department stores Bullock's Wilshire, the Ohrbach's chain, and Halls in Kansas City, to hotels, offices, country clubs, and private homes. He worked in a wide range of styles to suit his clients' needs, but his penchant for luxury was favored by such Hollywood elite as Gary Cooper, Cary Grant, and Barbara Stanwyck, and led to his reputation as a designer to the stars. As László explained, "I try to give the modern style an ageless importance, to be a little ahead of my time and yet build a comfortable home."[1] At the same time, he translated his opulent taste and generous proportions to mass-produced furniture, designing for such manufacturers as Rattan Stylists, Pacific Iron Products, Herman Miller Furniture Company, Ficks Reed, and Brown-Saltman. László also had a visionary side, designing bomb shelters and a hypothetical future city called Atomville, in which each subterranean house was sheltered from a nuclear blast and had its own swimming pool and helicopter landing strip. BT

1.
Paul László Collection, Architecture and Design Collection,
Art, Design & Architecture Museum.

Sources
· Paul László Collection, Architecture and Design
Collection, Art, Design & Architecture Museum,
University of California, Santa Barbara.
· Paul László, *Paul László* (Zurich: Conzett &
Huber, n.d.).

Olga Lee
b. 1924

A native of Los Angeles, Olga Lee designed modern furniture, textiles, lighting, and interiors. After graduating from high school in 1943, Lee worked at the Lockheed aircraft plant in Burbank making airplane dashboard assemblies. Following World War II, she enrolled at Chouinard Art Institute, where she studied art and design and met Milo Baughman—her future husband and design partner—in a furniture, interior, and set design class. Lee and Baughman shared a contemporary design aesthetic and an admiration of work produced at the Bauhaus. From 1948 to 1949 she worked in the design department at Barker Brothers, the vast downtown L.A. furniture emporium. In late 1951 the couple opened Baughman-Lee, a design shop on La Cienega Boulevard that sold textiles and wallpaper designed by Lee and furniture designed by Baughman, in addition to offering a full range of decorating services. Lee's work during this period is characterized by geometric patterns and vivid color. Both her *Elements* textile, produced by New York manufacturer L. Anton Maix, and a wasp-waisted lamp, one of a line of table and floor models made by the Ralph O. Smith Company in Burbank, were shown at the 1952 *Good Design* exhibition at MoMA. Although Baughman and Lee divorced in 1954, they continued to collaborate on projects. Lee moved to Chicago in 1957, where she designed showrooms, furnishings, and the interiors of several large hotels for furniture manufacturer Arch Gordon. BT

Sources
- Marilyn Hoffman, "California Designer of Furniture Keeps Considerate Eye on Customer," *Christian Science Monitor*, September 10, 1952.
- "California Newcomer," *Interiors*, May 1952, 102–3, 165.
- Study files, Balch Art Research Library, LACMA, DEC.002.

Olga Lee and Milo Baughman.

Malcolm Leland
b. 1922

Working as both a designer and artist over his long career, Malcolm Leland applied his modernist aesthetic and production expertise to home accessories, architectural elements, and large-scale public sculpture. In addition to designing utilitarian objects produced by Architectural Pottery in the 1950s, Leland was a prolific sculptor in clay, bronze, aluminum, and other materials, and created rhythmic ceramic and cast-concrete facades for many modern buildings. Born in Pasadena, he studied at Yale University School of Art, USC, and Jepson Art Institute in Los Angeles. In the early 1950s he designed and made a line of terracotta home accessories under the name Malcolm Leland Ceramics, and his biomorphic bird shelter was shown in the 1955 *Good Design* exhibition at MoMA. Leland licensed these designs to Architectural Pottery, which successfully produced them for many years. After a critical meeting with Richard Neutra in 1958, Leland was commissioned to design the cast-concrete facade of the architect's Los Angeles County Hall of Records, launching his career as an architectural sculptor. He worked closely with architects to design integral parts of many building facades, including the American Cement Company in Los Angeles and the San Diego Museum of Art. An active member of the California design community, he taught methods and materials at Chouinard Art Institute (1959–67) and exhibited work at every *California Design* exhibition, from his early slip-cast ceramics to later architectural elements such as cast doors and handles. ʙᴛ

Sources
· Norwood Teague, "Malcolm Leland on Sculpturing in Concrete," *Creative Crafts*, July/August 1962, 18–23.
· Study files, Balch Art Research Library, LACMA, DEC.002.

Levi Strauss & Co.
founded 1853

Established as a dry-goods wholesaler in San Francisco by Bavarian immigrant Levi Strauss (1829–1902), "Levi's" is now synonymous with the copper-riveted "waist overalls" manufactured as workwear since 1873—a California product that has become a staple and a symbol of American fashion. Strauss patented the process for riveting the stress points on men's pants with tailor Jacob Davis. Even though the 1906 San Francisco earthquake and fire destroyed its headquarters and factories, the company endured and continued to operate as a wholesaler and manufacturer (the wholesale business was discontinued around 1949). The Levi's name was trademarked in 1928. In the 1930s, as dude ranches grew popular among vacationers, the company began to expand the market for its waist overalls ("jeans" did not enter the American lexicon until the 1950s). *Dude Ranch Duds* was the company's first Western-wear line in the mid-1930s; *Lady Levi's* were also introduced, though not as workwear but for leisure. The Golden Gate International Exposition (1939–40) provided an opportunity to market to an even wider audience. To the delight of GGIE visitors, the company presented a mechanical rodeo in Vacationland with puppets clad in miniature versions of the garments, forging a link between the brand and the American cultural icon of the cowboy. After World War II, the firm expanded distribution across the United States (prior to this, most sales were limited to the west) and beyond and increasingly emphasized leisure clothing for the entire family. Still headquartered in San Francisco, Levi Strauss & Co. is now a global company with international production and distribution. JMM

Sources
- Levi Strauss & Co. Archives, San Francisco.
- Lynn Downey, *Images of America: Levi Strauss & Co.* (Charleston, S.C.: Arcadia, 2007).
- Lynn Downey, Jill Novack Lynch, and Kathleen McDonough, *This Is a Pair of Levi's Jeans . . . The Official History of the Levi's Brand* (San Francisco: Levi Strauss & Co., 1995).
- Walter A. Haas Sr., Daniel E. Koshland Sr., Walter A. Haas Jr., and Peter E. Haas, "Levi Strauss & Co.: Tailors to the World," interviews by Harriet Nathan, 1976, Regional Oral History Office, Bancroft Library, University of California, Berkeley.

LEVI'S CALIFORNIA

RANCH PANTS

Only California's own Levi Strauss has the feel and the flair to tailor these figure-flattering, slim-trim slacks with a cowboy-inspired silhouette. Three fabulous styles—Classic, Ivy and Sawtooth (with an intriguing zig-zag at pockets and seams). All the colors of the rainbow...and all washable! About $4.95 to $11.95.

Solids—in denim, cotton gabardine, pinwale corduroy, cavalry twill, chino twill, Sanforlan flannel and polished cotton.

Muted stripes in LEVI'S exclusive Verti-stripe denim.

Gay and bold stripes in denim, Army twill and polished cotton.

Fancy prints in pinwale corduroy.

Color-coordinated cotton shirts...about $4.95 to $5.95

LEVI'S
CALIFORNIA
RANCH PANTS
SANFORIZED

At better stores everywhere, or write LEVI STRAUSS of California • 98 Battery Street, San Francisco 6

Advertisement for Levi Strauss & Co. *California Ranch Pants*, 1950s.

Dorothy Wright Liebes
1899–1972

Famously called the "first lady of the loom," Dorothy Wright Liebes created vibrant textile designs and popularized the colorful aesthetic known as "The California Look." A native of Santa Rosa, Liebes experimented with weaving during her years at San Jose State Teachers College and the University of California, Berkeley, and studied the craft briefly at Hull House in Chicago before earning a degree from Teachers College of Columbia University. Back in San Francisco, she began her career as a studio weaver, founding Dorothy Liebes Design, Inc., in the 1930s. Her work became renowned for its intense, unconventional color combinations and richly textured surfaces, the result of using unorthodox materials such as ribbon, bamboo, ticker tape, and metal thread. She garnered the attention of many noted decorators and architects, receiving commissions from Gardner Dailey, Timothy Pflueger, and Frank Lloyd Wright, as well as many for public buildings and private homes. In the late 1930s Liebes began working as a designer and color consultant for textile, garment, and fiber manufacturers, bringing her distinctive look to mass production. She expanded her ties to the industry after relocating to New York in 1948, designing for E. I. du Pont de Nemours & Company and Goodall Fabrics, among others. In addition to her textile business, Liebes was an enthusiastic promoter of the applied arts and her fellow craftspeople; she served as director of decorative arts at the Golden Gate International Exposition (1939–40) and as national director of the Arts and Skills Project of the American Red Cross in 1943. Her work was represented in numerous exhibitions, including a retrospective at the Museum of Contemporary Crafts (1970), and she was honored with countless awards, from first prize in the category of American textiles at the Paris International Exposition (1937) to a posthumous gold medal from the American Craft Council (1975). JMM

Sources
- Dorothy Liebes Papers, 1925–1973, Archives of American Art, Smithsonian Institution.
- Alexandra Griffith Winton, "'None of Us Is Sentimental about the Hand': Dorothy Liebes, Handweaving, and Design for Industry," *The Journal of Modern Craft* 4, no. 3 (November 2011): 251–267.
- Alexandra Griffith Winton, "Color and Personality: Dorothy Liebes and American Design," *Archives of American Art Journal* 48, no. 1–2 (Spring 2009): 4–17.
- Regina Lee Blaszczyk, "Designing Synthetics, Promoting Brands: Dorothy Liebes, DuPont Fibres and Post-war American Interiors," *Journal of Design History* 21, no. 1 (July 2008): 75–99.

James Lovera

b. 1920

Ceramist James Lovera creates refined bowls with delicate walls and tactile, luminous glazes. His textures and colors are inspired by both natural forms and Chinese porcelains. Lovera, who was born in San Lorenzo, California, studied ceramics at the California School of Fine Arts (BA, 1942). His student work attracted the interest of Ernest Amberg, who became his mentor and introduced him to contemporary ceramics at Amberg-Hirth, the influential San Francisco gallery. Lovera met many important ceramists when he demonstrated throwing at the 1940 Art in Action display at the Golden Gate International Exposition (1939–40), where his work was also shown in the student section. In 1945 he was hired to research clay bodies and glazes for the California Pottery Company and worked under Marguerite Wildenhain. From 1946 through the 1950s he made small-production wares, developing a successful line of slip-cast birds and thrown functional work that was sold at Gump's department store in San Francisco. Lovera spent most of his career at San Jose State University, where he taught ceramics from 1948 to 1986. By the 1960s he had shifted his focus to unique work as the best expression for his inveterate experiments in glaze chemistry. Specializing in bowl forms whose open surfaces best displayed his glazes, Lovera was most inspired by Song dynasty ceramics and the texture of lichens and rocks. His ceramics have been included in a three-man exhibition at the M. H. de Young Museum in San Francisco (1960), numerous *Ceramic National Exhibitions* in Syracuse, *California Design 9* (1965), and *California Design 10* (1968). In 2006 the Crocker Art Museum in Sacramento organized *Craters from Fire*, a retrospective of his work. ss

Sources
· Diana L. Daniels and Robert D. Mowry, *Craters from Fire: Ceramics by James Lovera*, exh. cat. (Sacramento: Crocker Art Museum, 2006).
· Sandra Leader, "James Lovera," *Ceramics Monthly*, October 1996, 45–48.
· James Lovera, *James Lovera: Joanne Rapp Gallery/ The Hand and the Spirit, October 1–31, 1993*, exh. cat. (Scottsdale, Ariz.: Joanne Rapp Gallery, 1993).

Glen Lukens
1887–1967

As the head of one of California's first university ceramics programs, Glen Lukens influenced a generation of students with his relentless material experimentation. A committed modernist who believed that crafts should augment, rather than imitate, machine-made wares, he created rugged earthenware vessels that were built by hand or on molds. Born in Missouri, Lukens became interested in clay while studying art education at Oregon State University, Corvallis. In 1923 he relocated to Fullerton, California, where he taught high school and junior college and made numerous trips to Death Valley to gather minerals for his glaze experiments. One of his discoveries—the formula for an elusive Egyptian blue faience glaze—established his reputation and earned him an invitation to teach at USC in 1933. Lukens soon became head of the newly founded ceramics department and also taught jewelry making. While his ceramics classes focused on molded and cast earthenware, he was among the earliest teachers in Southern California to demonstrate wheel throwing. Several of his students later forged paths as leading ceramists and teachers in their own right, including F. Carlton Ball, Vivika Heino, and Harrison McIntosh, while others, notably architect Frank Gehry and jeweler Sam Kramer, earned acclaim in other fields. Over time Lukens's work shifted from the intense hues of his early glazes to earthier pieces whose crackled and unglazed surfaces evoked their desert origins. In the early 1940s he began experimenting with glass, slumping the material over ceramic molds to create translucent plates and chargers. An energetic advocate for his craft, Lukens wrote articles, performed public demonstrations, organized exhibitions, and applied his expertise to national and international efforts. During World War II he taught pottery as therapy for veterans and worked with his USC students to find a ceramic alternative to metal cookware, which was rationed during wartime. In 1945 Lukens went to Haiti as part of an Inter-American Education Council program to help develop that country's ceramics industry, a venture that occupied him through the 1950s. When he returned to the United States, he found that the field had shifted toward wheel-thrown, high-fire ceramics, leaving him in relative obscurity. Subsequent generations have rediscovered Lukens, beginning with a 1982 retrospective at California State University, Los Angeles. ss

Sources
- Glen Lukens Papers, 1931–1983, Archives of American Art, Smithsonian Institution.
- Elaine Levin, *Glen Lukens: Pioneer of the Vessel Aesthetic*, exh. cat. (Los Angeles: California State University, 1982).
- Study files, Balch Art Research Library, LACMA, DEC.002.

Alvin Lustig
1915–1955

In a prolific but tragically abbreviated career, Alvin Lustig—a teacher and mentor to an entire generation of designers—applied his innovative design approach to book jackets, logos, magazines, textiles, furniture, interiors, and architecture. Primarily self-taught, Lustig studied briefly at Taliesin with Frank Lloyd Wright and at Art Center School with Kem Weber. In his initial forays into graphic design in the late 1930s, he used printing ornaments to make elaborate geometric patterns for invitations, announcements, and books. A card for Jake Zeitlin's renowned bookstore led to an introduction to James Laughlin, founder of New Directions Publishing, who would become an important client and lifelong friend. The arresting jackets Lustig designed for contemporary fiction and poetry established his reputation. In 1942 he redesigned the logo and layout for *Arts and Architecture* magazine, an important example of the synergy between progressive architecture and graphic design. Recruited to be visual research director of *Look* magazine, Lustig moved to New York in 1944. He returned to Los Angeles two years later to work as a freelance designer and to teach at Art Center School. There Lustig exerted profound influence on dozens of designers who remember him for his inspired instruction, his advocacy for the breakdown of barriers between design disciplines, and his philosophy about the integration of design and life. Louis Danziger, John Follis, Rex Goode, Charles Kratka, and Frederick A. Usher Jr. are just a few of his many students who would later shape their fields. Lustig returned to New York in 1951, where he freelanced and served as a visiting critic at Yale University. He organized and designed a retrospective exhibition of his work in 1949 that opened at the A-D Gallery in New York and traveled around the country. Only a few months before his death from diabetes, the exhibition *Two Graphic Designers: Bruno Munari and Alvin Lustig* opened at MoMA. Lustig, who wrote that "something flies into your mind when the magic phrase 'California Modern' is uttered," was one of the key figures responsible for the distinctive nature of modern California design.[1] BT

1.
Alvin Lustig, "California Modern," *Designs*,
October 1947, 8.

Sources
- Alvin Lustig Papers, Graphic Design Archive,
  Rochester Institute of Technology, New York.
- Alvin Lustig Papers, Archives of American Art,
  Smithsonian Institution.
- Steven Heller and Elaine Lustig Cohen, *Born Modern:
  The Life and Design of Alvin Lustig* (San Francisco:
  Chronicle Books, 2010).
- Alvin Lustig and Holland R. Melson, eds., *The
  Collected Writings of Alvin Lustig* (New Haven,
  Conn.: H. R. Melson Jr., 1958).
- Alvin Lustig 1915–1955: Modern Design Pioneer
  (website), www.alvinlustig.org.

Peter Macchiarini
1909–2001

Best known for his sculptural approach to jewelry and use of layered planes of contrasting metals, Peter Macchiarini championed the creation of jewelry by hand over mass production and claimed never to have created two pieces exactly alike; he passionately advocated a clear distinction between handcrafted and mass-produced work, particularly in retail settings. Macchiarini was born in Sonoma County and traveled with his parents to their native Italy in 1924, where he studied clay modeling, architectural drawing, and marble cutting at the Art Academy in Pietrasanta, Tuscany. In 1928 he returned to the United States and worked as a stone carver in San Francisco while taking night courses at the California School of Fine Arts. He joined the Works Progress Administration in 1935 and was assigned to the Federal Theatre Project. After a few years, he was transferred to the Federal Art Project and worked under sculptors Beniamino Bufano and Ralph Stackpole. Inspired by readings about the Bauhaus and the work of Margaret De Patta, Macchiarini learned metalsmithing and began making jewelry in the 1930s. His studio and gallery opened its doors in San Francisco's North Beach district in 1948 and became a gathering place for avant-garde artists and craftspeople. A founding member of the Metal Arts Guild, he exhibited in many museum-sponsored solo and group shows, and his work is held in several public and private collections. Beginning in 1939, Macchiarini became an active proponent of outdoor art festivals and frequently participated as both organizer and exhibitor. JMM

Sources
· Ginger Moro, "The Outsider Turns Inward: Peter Macchiarini: Sculptor, Modernist Studio Jeweler, and Bohemian," *Echoes* 8, no. 3 (Winter 1999): 52–57, 74–77.
· Peter Macchiarini, interview by Mary McChesney, October 18, 1964, Archives of American Art, Smithsonian Institution.

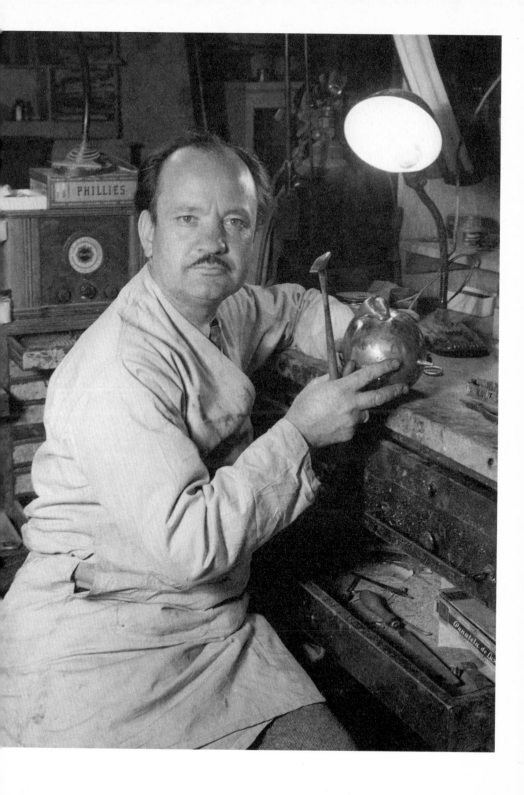

Strother MacMinn
1918–1998

Strother MacMinn taught transportation design at Art Center School for forty-six years, guiding the program to international dominance in the field. MacMinn was a teenager in Pasadena when he discovered his passion for automotive design, and he developed his portfolio under the mentorship of prominent custom car designer Franklin Hershey. Hershey helped him land a job in Detroit, where MacMinn spent four years working for car-industry giant Harley Earl, a California native whose legendary Art and Color department at General Motors established the field of automotive styling in the late 1920s. MacMinn soon tired of industry bureaucracy, however, and after serving in World War II returned to Pasadena to work for industrial designer Henry Dreyfuss. MacMinn began teaching at Art Center School in 1948, the same year that transportation design became an official major within the industrial design department. He set the standard for training in the field, running his courses like a professional design studio and incorporating the industry's latest processes and technologies. Though some questioned the direct link between education and vocation, industry leaders expressed their approval by hiring his students for competitive positions. At the time of MacMinn's death, his eulogists estimated that one-third of all important American automotive designers had trained with him. Beyond the classroom, he contributed regularly to *Motor Trend*, *Road & Track*, and other publications and played an instrumental role in founding Toyota's Calty Design Research studio in Newport Beach. Largely because of MacMinn's efforts, Southern California continues to be a hub of advanced car design. ss

Sources
- WM A. Motta, "Strother MacMinn," *Road & Track*, May 1998, 105, 107.
- Preston Lerner, "One for the Road," *Los Angeles Times*, February 9, 1992.
- Anna Ganahl, "Still Car Crazy After All These Years," *Abridged: A Publication for Art Center Alumni*, Fall 1991, 4–5.

Strother MacMinn with Art Center School students, 1960.

Sam Maloof
1916–2009

An exemplar and advocate of the craftsman lifestyle, Sam Maloof made furniture renowned for its organic and ergonomic forms and beautiful, lustrous woods. Born in Chino to Lebanese immigrant parents, this largely self-taught craftsman learned woodworking in the workshop of designer Harold Graham while pursuing a career as a graphic artist. After serving in World War II, Maloof began building furniture for his family as a hobby. He quit his job as a studio assistant to Millard Sheets soon after he received his first furniture commission and became a full-time maker, supported by the business acumen of his wife and manager, Alfreda Maloof (1911–1998). His first clients, notably William Manker and Henry Dreyfuss, were local, but early interest from *House Beautiful* and regular exhibitions soon attracted national attention. In 1953 Maloof moved to pastoral Alta Loma, building a home and studio that became a pilgrimage site for woodworkers. His mounting commissions allowed him to hire his first shop assistant in 1962; he maintained a small workshop for the remainder of his career. Maloof developed a range of templates but hand-shaped each piece. As a result, his overall aesthetic remained consistent, but his forms slowly evolved from the angular joints of his early work—made primarily in walnut—to the graceful curves and exotic woods that defined his mature furniture, especially his signature rocking chair. Notable among his many honors are a MacArthur Fellowship ("genius grant") in 1985, the first given to a craftsman, and a retrospective at the Renwick Gallery, Smithsonian Institution, in 2001. ss

Sources
- Harold B. Nelson, *The House That Sam Built: Sam Maloof and Art in the Pomona Valley, 1945–1985* (San Marino, Calif.: Huntington Library, Art Collections, and Botanical Gardens, 2011).
- Edward S. Cooke Jr., "The Long Shadow of William Morris: Paradigmatic Problems of Twentieth-Century American Furniture," in *American Furniture 2003*, ed. Luke Beckerdite (Milwaukee: Chipstone Foundation; Hanover, N.H.: University Press of New England, 2003).
- Jeremy Adamson, *The Furniture of Sam Maloof* (Washington, D.C.: Smithsonian American Art Museum; New York: Norton, 2001).
- Sam Maloof, *Sam Maloof, Woodworker* (New York: Kodansha International, 1989).

William Manker
1902–1997

Ceramist, educator, and stylist William Manker was renowned for his astute color sensibility reflected in both his ceramic glazes and his interior design. Originally from Upland, Manker studied at Chouinard Art Institute and began his career in 1924 as a designer for tilemaker Ernest Batchelder, a leader of the Arts and Crafts movement. After Batchelder's company went out of business, Manker opened William Manker Ceramics in 1932 in Pasadena, producing functional slip-cast pottery forms glazed in vivid colors. As the business grew, employees were hired to do the slip-casting while Manker designed the shapes and formulated glazes. In 1935 Millard Sheets hired him to establish a ceramics program at Scripps College in Claremont, and Manker soon opened a second studio in nearby Padua Hills. Manker learned to throw on the wheel in classes with Gertrud Natzler in 1938. From 1940 to 1945 he taught at both Claremont Graduate School and Scripps College and initiated the series of exhibitions that would become the *Scripps College Ceramic Annuals*. Manker was known for his refined forms and the subtle, brilliant colors of his glazes, particularly his oxblood and crackle glazes inspired by Asian ceramics. A frequent exhibitor and juror at the Los Angeles County Fair, he also showed widely and sold his pieces in shops nationwide. Manker reduced his teaching commitments around 1945 and closed his pottery studio in 1948 to devote more time to his design and color consultancy, including a position as color stylist for *House Beautiful*. JMM

Sources
· Sam Maloof, interview by Mary MacNaughton, January 10–11, 2002, Archives of American Art, Smithsonian Institution.
· Mary Davis MacNaughton, *Art at Scripps: The Early Years*, exh. cat. (Claremont: Galleries of the Claremont Colleges, 1988), 16.

Maurice Martiné
1918–2006

Corona del Mar–based furniture and interior designer Maurice Martiné created practical and affordable furnishings for modern homes out of readily available, inexpensive materials. Fashioned from a combination of steel, wood, wire, and cord, Martiné's light, airy furniture was sold through his company, Maurice Martiné Designs. A highly publicized 1948 group of chairs appealed to consumers with its innate simplicity: requiring only a screwdriver for assembly, the chairs could easily be constructed at home. As a contemporary *Arts and Architecture* article explained, "It is the plan of the designer that this furniture be purchased in a store and carried out under the customer's arm."[1] They were versatile, too—on the same wooden frame, customers could choose either a side chair or an armchair, and a cord or dowel seat. Another of his 1948 chair designs, which George Nelson described as "violen[t] in the comparison between the light wire frame and bold, sharp seat and back forms,"[2] received a first-place furniture award from the American Institute of Decorators, and two were included in *Chairs*, Nelson's influential 1953 compendium of contemporary design. Martiné continued to design furniture for several decades, creating chairs primarily of enameled steel tube, aluminum, cane, rosewood, or leather and tabletops of Formica, wood, and cork. Well known in the 1940s and 1950s, Martiné also collaborated with several architects on interior design projects, and his furniture was publicized in the magazines *Arts and Architecture* and *Interiors*. LS

1.
"Chairs by Maurice Martine,"
Arts and Architecture, 28.
2.
George Nelson, *Chairs* (1953; repr., New York:
Acanthus Press, 1994), 28.

Sources
- "Chairs by Maurice Martine," *Arts and Architecture*,
December 1948, 28.
- Study files, Balch Art Research Library, LACMA,
DEC.002.

Maurice Martiné for Maurice Martiné Designs, Chair, 1948.
LACMA, Gift of Daniel Morris and Denis Gallion, Courtesy of Historical Design, Inc.

Addie Masters
1901–1983

Brightly hued, upscale "at-home" apparel inspired by the patio lifestyle of Southern California was the trademark of Los Angeles fashion designer Addie Masters. Addie Masters Manufacturing, her business for home leisure and entertaining fashions, opened in 1940 and was managed by her husband, Albert R. Earle (1901–1949). Known for her luxurious, wide-legged hostess pajamas, the designer used supple fabrics such as rayon crepe and unusual combinations of bold colors in all-season garments that were both comfortable and glamorous. She brought ease and versatility to day dresses in sunny colors and prints. Her famous "wrap rascal," a dress in figure-conscious jersey that wrapped around the body and fastened at the waist, is imitated to this day. A member of the Affiliated Fashionists of California (see Louella Ballerino), Masters worked with fellow California designers to promote "The California Look" to a national audience and was honored as a legend of California fashion by the trade organization Los Angeles Fashion Group in 1976. JMM

Sources
- "Continued Use of Color and Color Contrasts Marks Addie Masters Year-'Round Designs," *Christian Science Monitor*, November 15, 1944.
- "Who Are the Real Designers . . . ," *California Stylist*, November 1940, 5.
- Study files, Balch Art Research Library, LACMA, DEC.002.

Mattel, Inc.
founded 1945

Ruth Handler (1916–2002) and Elliot Handler (1918–2011)—childhood sweethearts from Denver who moved to California in the late 1930s—launched toy manufacturing giant Mattel Creations with their friend Harold "Matt" Matson in a Los Angeles garage. (The name was a combination of *Matt* and *El*liot.) Matson sold his interest in the company shortly thereafter, and Mattel was incorporated in 1948 with headquarters in Hawthorne. While Mattel's first products were picture frames, the company soon began making dollhouse furniture from the leftover scraps and developed a specialty in toy manufacturing. The first successes were musical: the Uke-A-Doodle and a patented hand-cranked music box. In 1955 Mattel became the first toy company to advertise on television year-round with the sponsorship of the new series *The Mickey Mouse Club*. This successful gamble revolutionized toy marketing by appealing directly to children and proved the potential for significant sales outside the Christmas season. In 1959 the company introduced Barbie, a doll that combined Hollywood glamour and the casual California lifestyle. With her mature body and sophisticated clothing, the "Teen Age Fashion Model" was a dramatic break from traditional baby dolls. She quickly became Mattel's best-selling product and the world's best-selling doll, with sales now in the billions. Barbie's success spawned several companion dolls, such as boyfriend Ken (1961), and innumerable accessories that included Barbie's Dream House (1962), all of which enhanced her aspirational appeal to young girls. By 1965 the Handlers' small business had grown into an international venture with over $100 million in sales. Today the largest toy company in the world, Mattel, Inc., is headquartered in El Segundo. JMM

Sources
- Ruth Handler Papers, Schlesinger Library, Radcliffe Institute, Harvard University, Cambridge, Massachusetts.
- Robin Gerber, *Barbie and Ruth: The Story of the World's Most Famous Doll and the Woman Who Created Her* (New York: HarperCollins, 2009).
- John W. Amerman, *The Story of Mattel, Inc.: Fifty Years of Innovation* (New York: Newcomen Society; Princeton, N.J.: Princeton Academic Press, 1995).
- Elliot Handler, *The Impossible Really Is Possible: The Story of Mattel* (New York: Newcomen Society; Princeton, N.J.: Princeton University Press, 1968).
- "Corporations: All's Swell at Mattel," *Time*, October 26, 1962.

Ruth and Elliot Handler.

Designer, photographer, and filmmaker Herbert Matter played a central role in introducing the visual vocabulary of European modernism to mainstream American advertising.
Through experimentation with photographic processes such as photomontage and
solarization, manipulation of form, contrasts in scale, and bold typographic elements,
he applied avant-garde techniques to advertisements, magazine layouts, and exhibition
design. Matter was born in Engelberg, Switzerland, and trained at the École des Beaux-
Arts (School of Fine Arts) in Geneva. He furthered his education in Paris with such
luminaries of art and design as Fernand Léger, Amédée Ozenfant, Le Corbusier, and
A. M. Cassandre. Matter worked as a photographer and typographer for the type foundry
Deberny and Peignot before returning to Switzerland in 1932 and producing an internationally acclaimed series of travel posters for the Swiss National Tourist Office. He
moved to New York City in 1935 and worked as a photographer for Condé Nast, creating
cover art, advertisements, and layouts for *Vogue* and *Harper's Bazaar*. At the invitation of
Charles Eames, Matter moved to California in 1943 to join the Eames Office, where he
was an in-house photographer and graphic designer for three years. Using montage,
abstract compositions, multiple exposures, and the close-up, his photographs of molded-
plywood furniture and parts uniquely captured the Eameses' experiments with new
materials and form. Recruited by Knoll Associates as designer and advertising consultant,
Matter left the Eames Office in 1946 and returned to New York. Significant clients
included *Arts and Architecture* magazine, for which he designed numerous covers, and
later the Guggenheim Museum. Matter taught photography and graphic design at Yale
University (1952–76) and received a gold medal from the AIGA in 1983. LS

Sources
· *The Visual Language of Herbert Matter*, directed
by Reto Caduff (Zurich, Switzerland: PiXiU Films,
2010), DVD.
· Jeffrey Head, *Herbert Matter: Modernist
Photography and Graphic Design* (Palo Alto:
Stanford University Press, 2005).

Combining aspects of both Eastern and Western ceramic traditions, Harrison McIntosh created elegantly proportioned stoneware vessels and sculpture ornamented with precise patterns drawn in muted engobes and sgraffito. McIntosh moved to Los Angeles from his native Vallejo in Northern California in 1937, following his brother to Art Center School. Inspired by the Japanese pottery he saw at the Golden Gate International Exposition (1939–40), he took night courses in ceramics with Glen Lukens and, after World War II, worked with Albert Henry King. From 1949 to 1952 he studied at Claremont Graduate School with Richard B. Petterson. In 1950 McIntosh set up a studio with fellow student Rupert Deese, where they shared space, glazes, and materials until 2006. McIntosh further developed his skills at the influential seminar taught by potters Bernard Leach, Shoji Hamada, and Soetsu Yanagi at Mills College (1952) and at a summer session with Marguerite Wildenhain at Pond Farm Pottery (1953). Primarily a studio potter and frequent participant in local and national ceramic and craft exhibitions, he also taught alongside Peter Voulkos at the Los Angeles County Art Institute in the late 1950s and designed for production at Interpace Ceramics (1964–66; see Gladding, McBean & Company) and Mikasa (1970–80), where he collaborated with his wife, Marguerite McIntosh (b. France, 1925), on ceramic and glass tableware. In the late 1960s he began making closed sculptural forms on wooden bases often made by Sam Maloof, which share the refined aesthetic of his vessels. McIntosh drew little distinction between these modes of working, commenting that "in the end, functional pieces and sculptures are and should remain very close in their main purpose, the exploration of form. There is no sculpture more abstract than a vase."[1] ss

1.
Masterworks (Beverly Hills: Louis Newman
Galleries, 1984), n.p.

Sources
- Harrison McIntosh Papers, 1962–2002, Archives of
American Art, Smithsonian Institution.
- Christy Johnson, Martha W. Longenecker-Roth, and
Marguerite McIntosh, *Harrison McIntosh: A Timeless
Legacy* (Pomona: American Museum of Ceramic
Art, 2009).
- Harrison McIntosh, interview by Mary MacNaughton,
February 2–March 4, 1999, Archives of American
Art, Smithsonian Institution.
- Garth Clark and Hazel Bray, *Harrison McIntosh:
Studio Potter* (Rancho Cucamonga, Calif.: Rex W.
Wignall Museum-Gallery, Chaffey Community
College, 1979).

Metlox Manufacturing Company was one of the "Big Five" California pottery manufacturers (see Gladding, McBean & Company) that offered vibrant, solid-color dinnerware to brighten Depression-era dining tables. Founded by inventors Theodore C. Prouty
(c. 1871–1931) and his son Willis Prouty (1897–1978), the Manhattan Beach company (the
name was an abbreviation of *metal oxide*) specialized in ceramic outdoor advertising signs
that served as weatherproof, insulated bases for neon tubing. After his father's death,
Willis recognized the need to diversify the product line to stay in business and converted
the company's facilities to dinnerware production. Metlox introduced its first pattern,
California Pottery, or the "100 Series," in 1932, followed by *Poppy Trail* (after the California state flower), or the "200 Series," in 1934, and then three more solid-color dinnerware lines before expanding into artware in 1938. Dinnerware and artware production
ceased during World War II. In 1946 Prouty sold Metlox to Evan K. Shaw, who turned
hand-painted dinnerware into the company's specialty, hiring former animators Bob Allen
and Mel Shaw as art directors and Frank Irwin as supervisor of model development.
Metlox products appealed to both modern and traditional tastes. Dynamic patterns such
as *California Contempora*, *California Aztec*, and *California Provincial* were hand-painted
on ceramic blanks, and the products were sold in sets or as open stock. In 1958 Metlox
bought Vernon Kilns, acquiring the rights to the Vernonware name as well as the molds,
equipment, and stock. JMM

Sources
· Carl Gibbs Jr., *Collector's Encyclopedia of Metlox
Potteries*, 2nd ed. (Paducah, Ky.: Collector Books,
2001).

TREND SETTING

California Freeform
DINNERWARE

...created for moderns who
want something different. Cocoa,
chartreuse and sharp yellow
against a background of palest
grey, "textured" with tiny
dots of color; decoration
of these novel designs is
painted by hand, then glazed,
to make this delightful
ware oven safe and
dishwasher proof.

Designed under the art direction of Allen & Shaw.

Poppy*trail* METLOX

The American   Style in Dinnerware

Metlox Manufacturing Company brochure, c. 1954.

Gertrud Natzler
1908–1971
Otto Natzler
1908–2007

Collaborators in both work and life, Gertrud and Otto Natzler received international acclaim for their graceful ceramic vessels. Their output was prolific: Gertrud excelled at throwing elegant, thin-walled bowls, vases, and vessel forms on the wheel, while Otto experimented intensively with glaze recipes and firing techniques to create his signature colorful Pompeian, crater, and crystalline glazes and reduction-fired effects. Born in Vienna, they took ceramics classes together briefly there in the 1930s. They soon established their own studio, purchasing equipment and materials and learning techniques through trial and error. Their pieces sold quickly in high-end Viennese gift shops, and their early work was acknowledged by a silver medal at the Paris International Exposition (1937). After the Nazi invasion of Austria in 1938, the Natzlers fled Vienna for Los Angeles, where Otto had relatives. The artists brought with them a small electric kiln and kick wheel, which they continued to use throughout most of their working lives and are now in the collection of the National Museum of American History at the Smithsonian Institution. Considered giants in the revived field of studio ceramics, the Natzlers were among a small number of potters represented by the prestigious L.A. gallery Dalzell Hatfield. Their work was included in dozens of national and international exhibitions over their long careers, and they received several retrospectives, including one at LACMA (1966) and a large-scale show at the Smithsonian's Renwick Gallery (1973). Following Gertrud's death, Otto continued to work, moving away from Gertrud's functionally inspired vessels and creating slab-constructed clay sculpture. BT

Sources
· Otto Natzler, interview by Ruth Bowman, July 7–14, 1980, Archives of American Art, Smithsonian Institution.
· Gertrud Natzler and Otto Natzler, *Form and Fire: Natzler Ceramics, 1939–1972*, exh. cat. (Washington, D.C.: Renwick Gallery, 1973).
· *Gertrud and Otto Natzler: Ceramics: Catalog of the Collection of Mrs. Leonard M. Sperry*, exh. cat. (Los Angeles: LACMA, 1968).

John Nicholas Otar
1891–1939

Santa Cruz–based metalworker John Nicholas Otar created sculptural handwrought lamps, screens, boxes, andirons, and other household fixtures in the 1920s and 1930s. Working in a range of styles—Art Deco, Spanish colonial, mission revival, Arts and Crafts—he created heavily filigreed copper, brass, and iron work for hotels, nightclubs, and homes throughout the Santa Cruz area. Born John Otaredze in Georgia, Russia, Otar came to the United States during World War I. After working in New Jersey for the Ordnance Engineering and Testing Company on experimental explosives, Otar relocated to Boston and learned metalworking and lamp making before moving west to San Francisco in 1919. Shortly thereafter he set up a metalworking studio in Santa Cruz and established a name for himself—"Otar the Lampmaker," as locals knew him—and a reputation for ornate hammered metalwork. Although his career was cut short by his untimely death at age forty-eight, he completed many private and public commissions during his sixteen years in Santa Cruz, among them grillwork, chandeliers, and wall sconces for the Rio del Mar Golf Lodge and Hotel in Aptos and a series of lamps for the Hawaiian Gardens nightclub in Capitola. LS

Sources
· Sarah Weston, "Otar's Magic Lamps,"
The Mid-County Post, January 9, 2007.
· Study files, Balch Art Research Library, LACMA,
DEC.002.

John Nicholas Otar, Covered box, c. 1933. LACMA, Decorative Arts Deaccession Fund.

Pacific Clay Products Company

founded c. 1891

Pacific Clay Products Company was one of several established California pottery companies to place a new emphasis on the production of dinnerware, kitchenware, and artware to cushion the drop in demand for building materials during the Great Depression. The company, formed from a series of mergers of California clay manufacturers, had churned out a variety of architectural products during the 1920s building boom. By the mid-1920s the company was producing utilitarian wares such as poultry feeders and crocks at its factory in the Lincoln Heights neighborhood of Los Angeles. Following the example of another "Big Five" manufacturer, J. A. Bauer Pottery Company (see also Gladding, McBean & Company), the pottery division of Pacific Clay Products Company—known as Pacific Pottery—introduced the *Hostess Ware* line in six vivid colors in 1932. The streamlined design and diversity of products for table and kitchen proved successful with consumers, who were encouraged to be adventurous in mixing and matching their table settings. To keep up with popular tastes, from 1935 Pacific introduced new pastel colors and decorated wares with hand-painted designs applied over the glaze of its solid-color pottery. Thinner, lighter-weight dinnerware lines were available starting in 1937. Changing consumer tastes, competition from Eastern manufacturers, restrictions on materials because of World War II, and the need for war supplies diminished the market for California solid-color pottery by the early 1940s. By October 1942 Pacific had shifted production to making steatite porcelain (often used as electrical insulation) for the government and was the only pottery of the "Big Five" that did not resume production of tableware after the war. Pacific Clay Products currently manufactures architectural clay products in Lake Elsinore. JMM

Sources
· Jeffrey B. Snyder, *Pacific Pottery: Tableware from the 1920s, '30s, '40s . . . and More!* (Atglen, Pa.: Schiffer, 2001).

From Colorful California

VIVID, ARRESTING POTTERY IN
SMART DINNER AND BUFFET SERVICES

In the rich, warm colors reminiscent of old Spain...yet styled to the modern mood...Pacific pottery brings the *fiesta* spirit to present day dining.

Whether it appears as the first cheerful note on the breakfast tray...as part of the color harmony of an informal lunch...a zestful background for buffet suppers...or even as a gala touch to more formal dinners...there's a subtle magic about these decorative pieces.

Pacific pottery is satin-smooth in texture. Heat and cold resistant. Designed for every serving need, at prices surprisingly moderate. Six appealing colors, Apache Red, Lemon Yellow, Delphinium Blue, Jade Green, Sierra White, Pacific Blue.

Sold at leading stores...Descriptive folder in colors available upon request

Pacific POTTERY

Division of PACIFIC CLAY PRODUCTS, *Los Angeles, California*

Pacific Clay Products Company advertisement, 1935.

Maynard L. Parker
1900–1976

Maynard L. Parker captured images of residential architecture, interiors, and gardens and disseminated them to a national audience through popular shelter magazines. Born and raised in New England, Parker taught himself photography in the 1920s and entered his early work in amateur competitions. After multiple trips west, he settled permanently in Los Angeles in 1929 and became a professional photographer in the early 1930s. He worked for Skinner's Art Gallery and the architectural photography firm Mott Studios before establishing Maynard L. Parker Fine Photographs in 1938 (renamed Maynard L. Parker Modern Photography in 1940) in L.A.'s Echo Park neighborhood. In the early 1940s Elizabeth Gordon, editor of *House Beautiful*, took an interest in his work, and Parker soon became well known for his dramatically lit, well-staged photographs of residential and landscape architecture, which were featured in *House Beautiful*, *Better Homes & Gardens*, *Architectural Digest*, and other wide-circulation home and garden periodicals. His extensive list of clients included celebrities, furnishing retailers, and California designers and architects such as Paul T. Frankl, Paul László, Cliff May, and Harwell Hamilton Harris, who was Parker's neighbor. He also traveled across the country documenting the work of the nation's foremost designers, landscape designers, and architects. Parker's photography career continued until the early 1970s. JMM

Sources
- Maynard L. Parker (negatives, photographs, and other material), the Huntington Library, Art Collections, and Botanical Gardens, San Marino, California.
- Jennifer A. Watts, ed., *Maynard L. Parker Modern Photography and the American Dream* (New Haven, Conn.: Yale University Press, 2012).

Please
Excuse our
upset condition
We are
PHOTOGRAPHING
PACIFICA
for House Beautiful
Magazine

Maynard Parker at Jacksons Furniture Store, Oakland, California, 1953.

A versatile silversmith and gregarious socialite, Philip Paval made hollowware, jewelry, and metal sculptures that blended elements of streamlining and moderne classicism and were inspired by the glossy surfaces and dramatic angles of cinema sets. Born Philip Kranker Petersen in Nykobing, Denmark, Paval completed a traditional goldsmithing and silversmithing apprenticeship, supplemented with technical courses in drawing. In 1919 he left Copenhagen, where he had been engaged in prosaic work in a silver factory and a repair shop, and traveled to New York as a merchant seaman. He remained in New Jersey doing jewelry repair, but his hunger for adventure and opportunity led him to Los Angeles in the 1920s. Within a few years he had opened his own shop, and his business grew so rapidly that he began to produce original designs in addition to doing repairs and reproductions. Paval's handwrought silver attracted Rudolph Valentino, Marion Davies, Elizabeth Taylor, and other elite Hollywood clients. An avid self-promoter, he successfully campaigned to have his work presented to visiting Danish royalty in 1939 and, as president of the California Art Club in the early 1950s, boosted the organization's profile by convincing Winston Churchill to become an honorary member. He achieved considerable success in the artistic community as well, selling his work through Dalzell Hatfield Galleries and exhibiting at national craft invitationals, the Pasadena Art Institute, and several group shows at the Los Angeles Museum of History, Science and Art (now LACMA), most notably in 1944, when the museum displayed twelve cases of his work. ss

Sources
· Alice Kaufman, "Philip Paval: Hollywood's Forgotten Man," *Silver Magazine*, March/April 2005, 32–37.
· Philip Paval, *Paval: Autobiography of a Hollywood Artist* (Hollywood: Gunther Press, 1968).
· Study files, Balch Art Research Library, LACMA, DEC.002.

In 1922 German architect Jock D. Peters immigrated to Los Angeles, bringing the rational geometric yet classicist style he had honed in his native country to the design of film sets, furnishings, and critically acclaimed shop and domestic interiors. Born in Jarrenwisch in northern Germany, Jakob (Jock) Detlef Peters worked for legendary architect and designer Peter Behrens before becoming director of the Government School of Allied Arts in Altona, Germany. After spending several years designing sets for Famous Players–Lasky and other Los Angeles film companies, he formed Peters Brothers Modern American Design with his brother George. His breakthrough project as an independent designer was the Bullock's Wilshire department store (1929; John and Donald Parkinson, architects). On the first three floors of the building, he created a distinct aesthetic for each department by using exotic woods, metals, and rich textiles that resulted in sensuous, modern spaces. Critics praised his innovative use of cork and aluminum as well as his unified design. Peters's attention to detail won the admiration of writer and arts advocate Pauline Gibling Schindler, who included Peters in her *Contemporary Creative Architects* exhibition at the California Art Club (1930) alongside better-known modernists such as Richard Neutra and her husband, R. M. Schindler. His work for Bullock's and his subsequent design for New York's L. P. Hollander Company Building were lauded by East Coast critics, but his career was cut short by his premature death. In an obituary, *Los Angeles Times* art critic Arthur Millier described Peters as a "modern designer of unusual clarity, charm and sincerity," noting that "he lavished as much care on the design of a clock or the tiniest metal ornament as on planning the large elements of wall or ceiling."[1] ss

1.
Arthur Millier, "Jock D. Peters,"
Los Angeles Times, June 10, 1934.

Sources
- Jakob (Jock) Detlef Peters Collection, Architecture and Design Collection, Art, Design & Architecture Museum, University of California, Santa Barbara.
- Victoria Dailey, Michael Dawson, and Natalie Shivers, *LA's Early Moderns* (Glendale: Balcony Press, 2003), 82–84.
- Ralph Flint, "Jock Peters," *Creative Art*, September 1932, 30–33.

Richard B. Petterson
1910–1996

Ceramist Richard B. Petterson was an influential educator and advocate for the Southern California craft community. At times collaborating with his wife, Alice, he worked in Lucite, wood, glass, and enamels, in addition to clay. Petterson was born in Los Angeles but grew up in Tientsin, China, and attended Pei Yang University before returning to Los Angeles to study design and crafts at UCLA, where he graduated with a teaching credential in 1938. He taught ceramics at Pasadena City College and directed a summer art program at the University of Chicago from 1941 to 1946. An exhibition of his ceramics at the Pasadena Art Museum (1947) resulted in an invitation from Millard Sheets to join the faculty at Scripps College in Claremont. During his tenure there, Petterson exposed students to prominent potters and new developments in the field, transforming the program to include wheel throwing and high-fire stoneware and porcelain clay bodies, as well as expanding the *Scripps College Ceramic Annual* exhibitions. In 1957 Petterson left Scripps to direct an arts program in Taiwan at the invitation of the U.S. State Department. He returned in 1960 to direct the galleries at Scripps. As a leader and promoter of California artists and craftspeople, he served as co-organizer and later as director of arts and crafts at the Los Angeles County Fair for thirty years. Richard and Alice's involvement in the organization and direction of an annual show of international arts and crafts at Pilgrim Place, a Claremont retirement community, culminated in the founding of the Petterson Museum of Intercultural Art in 1983, named in recognition of the couple's contributions. JMM

Sources
- Victor J. Danilov, "Petterson Museum of Intercultural Art," in *Women and Museums: A Comprehensive Guide* (Lanham, Md.: AltaMira Press, 2005), 124–25.
- Mary Davis MacNaughton, *Art at Scripps: The Early Years*, exh. cat. (Claremont: Galleries of the Claremont Colleges, Scripps College, Pomona College, 1987).

(From left) Arthur and Jean Ames, Richard B. and Alice Petterson,
and Phil and Betty Dike, c. 1955.

Antonio Prieto
1912–1967

Influenced by the abstract forms of European modernism, ceramist and teacher Antonio Prieto created stoneware vessels and sculptures characterized by distinctive sgraffito glyphs and earth-toned engobe glazes. Prieto emigrated from Spain to the United States as an infant; he and his family settled first in Hawaii and then in Chico, California. In 1940 Prieto moved to San Francisco, where he took adult education classes in sculpture at the California School of Fine Arts and experimented with clay as a charter member of the Mills College Ceramic Guild established by F. Carlton Ball. After serving in World War II, he studied at Alfred University in New York and returned west to teach at CCAC in 1946. Prieto reconnected with Ball in Oakland, eventually succeeding him as chairman of the ceramics department at Mills College in 1950 and becoming head of the art department in 1957. An active proponent of the craft movement, Prieto was selected as a representative to the First Conference of Potters and Weavers in Britain (1952) and was one of the first craftsman trustees of the American Craft Council. Although his work remained formally tied to traditional vessels, he acknowledged that his intent was more artistic than utilitarian and that he created only unique works. He stopped short, however, of accepting the radical forms of artists like Peter Voulkos, a distinction that drove a wedge between Prieto and his most famous student, sculptor Robert Arneson. A frequent traveler in his later years, Prieto received a Fulbright fellowship to research village potters in Spain (1963–64). Mills College assembled the Antonio Prieto Collection of Ceramics as a memorial to him, with contributions from more than one hundred artists. ss

Sources
· Antonio Prieto Papers, 1947–1967, Archives of American Art, Smithsonian Institution.
· Susan Peterson, "Antonio Prieto 1912–1967," *Craft Horizons*, July/August 1967, 23–25.

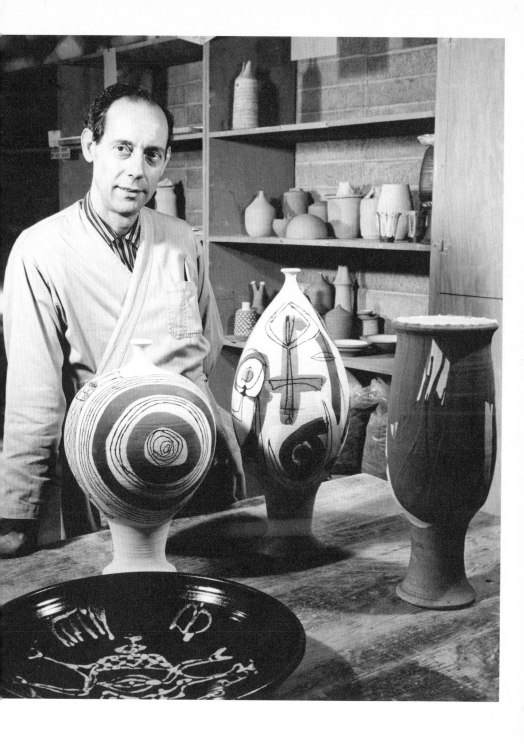

Myrton Purkiss
1912–1978

For ceramist Myrton Purkiss, clay was a medium for artistic expression. To him the vessel was a canvas, and his works were intended to grace walls rather than serve as containers. Originally from Victoria, British Columbia, Purkiss moved to Southern California as a child and graduated from Fullerton High School, where he first studied ceramics with Glen Lukens. After completing coursework at Chouinard Art Institute, Purkiss again studied with Lukens, this time at USC. He opened a pottery studio in Fullerton in 1938 and exhibited both locally and nationally. World War II intervened, and he spent three years in the Army Corps of Engineers. After the war, Purkiss studied ceramics in England and France before returning to Fullerton and his studio. Using a maiolica (tin-glazed earthenware) technique, he created plate and bowl forms using loosely rendered floral and fruit motifs or complex, abstract designs in a broad array of colors. His work was sold exclusively through Dalzell Hatfield Galleries in Los Angeles and was exhibited in several *Ceramic National Exhibitions* in Syracuse, the *Scripps College Ceramic Annuals*, and the *Pacific Coast Ceramic Exhibitions*. A large decorated bowl was included in *6000 Years: Art in Clay*, an exhibition organized by Millard Sheets and Richard B. Petterson at the 1952 Los Angeles County Fair. Purkiss ended his ceramics career in the mid-1950s because of diminishing demand and in 1954 began to work as a landscape architect. A retrospective of his work was held at the Muckenthaler Cultural Center in Fullerton (1977). JMM

Sources
- James Normile, *Myrton Purkiss: Modern Ceramics*, exh. cat. (Los Angeles: Dalzell Hatfield Galleries, 1952).
- Study files, Balch Art Research Library, LACMA, DEC.002.

Ruth Radakovich
1920–1975

Jeweler, sculptor, and designer Ruth Radakovich adopted a language of organic form and often used semiprecious stones and minerals in gravity-defying settings in her jewelry and metalwork. Born Ruth Clark, Radakovich attended Sarah Lawrence College and the University of Michigan (MA, 1949). She also studied pottery and jewelry with F. Carlton Ball at Mills College and ceramics and metalwork at the School for American Craftsmen in Rochester, New York. Ruth met Svetozar (Toza) Radakovich in 1946 while working for the United Nations Relief and Rehabilitation Administration in Toza's native Belgrade. She returned to the United States soon after, but they were reunited in Europe in the early 1950s and married in Paris in 1954. Before returning to the United States, they studied with silversmith Mogens Bjørn-Andersen in Copenhagen. The Radakoviches settled in Rochester in 1955, where Ruth made jewelry and metalwork and taught at the Memorial Art Gallery for three years. In 1956 she received the coveted Hickok Award for "excelling design and craftsmanship" at the *Second Exhibition of American Jewelry and Related Objects* at the Memorial Art Gallery. Her prize-winning gold and turquoise pin appeared on the cover of *Craft Horizons* in February of the following year. Ruth and Toza moved to Encinitas, north of San Diego, in 1959 and became part of the fledgling San Diego arts community. They worked independently of each other, although they exchanged ideas and shared tools. Primarily a jeweler but, like Toza, an inveterate experimenter in many materials, Ruth was inspired by forms found in nature, including leaves, seedpods, and shells scavenged on trips to the beach near her home. She frequently exhibited her work in the *California Design* exhibitions and at the Brussels World's Fair (1958). Ruth and Toza were the subject of shows at the Albright Art Gallery (1959), the Long Beach Museum of Art (1961), and both the Santa Barbara Museum of Art and the Pasadena Art Museum (1962). BT

Sources
· Toni Greenbaum, "Svetozar and Ruth Radakovich: Love in Three Dimensions," *Metalsmith* 27, no. 3 (2007): 34–41.
· Arline Fisch, "Ruth Radakovich, 1920–1975," *Craft Horizons*, April 1975, 6.
· "Radakovich," *Craft Horizons*, September/ October 1958, 24–31.
· Bernice Stevens Decker, "Couple Link Skills," *Christian Science Monitor*, August 28, 1958.

Ruth and Svetozar (Toza) Radakovich.

Svetozar (Toza) Radakovich
1918–1998

Svetozar (Toza) Radakovich made jewelry and objects in wood, metal, and plastic that often combined sculptural form with functional purpose. He received an MA in fine arts from the Royal Academy of Art in his native Belgrade, in the former Yugoslavia, and began his career as a painter. After being imprisoned as a POW during World War II, he worked for the United Nations Relief and Rehabilitation Administration in Belgrade, where he met his future wife, Ruth Radakovich. Toza and Ruth married in 1954, and they studied with silversmith Mogens Bjørn-Andersen in Copenhagen—Toza's first experience working in metal—before arriving in the United States in 1955. They settled in Rochester, New York, where Toza pursued metalworking and taught art and design at the School for American Craftsmen, the Rochester Institute of Technology, and the Memorial Art Gallery. Wanting to live near the ocean and in a warm climate that would allow them to work outside year-round, the Radakoviches moved west to Encinitas, near San Diego, in 1959. While Ruth and Toza generally maintained separate bodies of work, they often exchanged ideas and shared their tools and materials. Toza worked in a wide variety of materials and scales, making jewelry, stained glass, metal sculpture, architectural elements, and even play-ground equipment. He became well known for his monumental doors made of sculpted wood and fiberglass. In the early 1960s he participated in the Southwest Indian arts program at the University of Arizona, where he was paired with Native American jeweler Charles Loloma and began incorporating Indian motifs into his work. Ruth and Toza received extensive critical acclaim and exhibited frequently throughout their careers. BT

Sources
· Toni Greenbaum, "Svetozar and Ruth Radakovich: Love in Three Dimensions," *Metalsmith* 27, no. 3 (2007): 34–41.
· "Radakovich," *Craft Horizons*, September/October 1958, 24–31.
· Bernice Stevens Decker, "Couple Link Skills," *Christian Science Monitor*, August 28, 1958.

Svetozar Radakovich with Carl Eckstrom, Double door, c. 1967.

Barney Reid
1913–1992

An active figure in San Diego's design community, Barney Reid was a versatile artist and craftsman who worked in jewelry, enamels, textiles, ceramics, wood, and works on paper. Raised in Yuma Valley, Arizona, Reid earned a BA from Arizona State College and studied with Grant Wood and Fletcher Martin at the State University of Iowa, where he completed his master's in lithography under Emil Ganso. In the late 1940s Reid moved to San Diego to work as an art director and graphic designer; he also briefly shared a studio with Harry Bertoia. One of the founding members of the Allied Craftsmen of San Diego, he began showing jewelry with the organization in 1951 and served as president beginning in 1953. His jewelry, mostly in enamel on copper, was featured in several national exhibitions in the 1950s and early 1960s, including *Designer Craftsmen U.S.A.* (1953), *American Jewelry and Related Objects* (1955), *Craftsmanship in a Changing World* (1956), and *Contemporary Craftsmen of the Far West* (1961). In about 1950 he started ReidArt, a textile screenprinting business located in the old Convair plant in San Diego. Characterized by abstract forms and vivid color, ReidArt's table linens and yardage were sold at Gump's department store in San Francisco and national retailers. The business proved to be short-lived, however, when the U.S. Navy reclaimed the building at the onset of the Korean War. Reid turned to metal sculpture in the 1960s and worked almost exclusively in intaglio printmaking from the late 1970s until his death. JMM

Sources
- Toni Greenbaum, "Tea and Jewelry: Modernist Metalsmithing in San Diego, 1940-1970," *Metalsmith* 22, no. 3 (Summer 2002): 26–33.
- Barney Reid, William B. Kelley, and Martin E. Petersen, *Man & Places & Things Happening: Intaglio Prints by Barney Reid* (San Diego: Brighton Press, 1987).

merry renk
1921–2012

San Francisco artist merry renk created modern jewelry forms using an abstracted language of interlocking, folded, and repeated shapes and kinetic elements in a range of materials that included sterling silver, gold, enamel, pearls, and semiprecious stones. She was born Mary Gibbs in Trenton, New Jersey, and studied painting at the School of Industrial Arts in Trenton. After her first husband died in combat in World War II, renk enrolled at the Institute of Design in Chicago, planning to support herself as an industrial designer. With two fellow students, she opened 750 Studio in 1947, which served as their residence and workshop. The women sold contemporary crafts, painting, sculpture, and photography, and renk began experimenting with enamel and bent wire. At that point she also decided that capitals and serifs were nonessential, and from then on spelled her name entirely in lowercase letters. She moved to San Francisco in 1948 and established a studio in her home. With her second husband, ceramist Earle Curtis, she developed a close circle of artist friends that included Ruth Asawa and Asawa's husband, architect Albert Lanier (renk's next-door neighbors), and photographer Imogen Cunningham, among others. One of the founding members of the Metal Arts Guild—a regular gathering of Bay Area metal artists—renk considered fellow member Margaret De Patta to have been a close friend and mentor. In 1967, after an accident resulted in the loss of sight in one eye, she turned to creating large-scale, interlocking sculptures. She resumed making jewelry once she adjusted to the change in her vision. Her later work incorporated a type of figurative imagery she called "symbolic realism," which often included natural motifs such as birds and leaves. Her work was widely shown in exhibitions at the M. H. de Young, the Smithsonian, and other museums, and she received a retrospective at the California Crafts Museum in Palo Alto in 1981. In 1983 she shifted her focus to watercolor painting and archiving her extensive career. JMM

Sources
- Merry Renk Papers, 1952–2000, Archives of American Art, Smithsonian Institution.
- Merry Renk, interview by Arline Fisch, January 18–19, 2001, Archives of American Art, Smithsonian Institution.
- Joan Pearson Watkins, "Opulent and Organic: The Jewelry of Merry Renk," *American Craft*, April/May 1981, 32–35.
- Merry Renk, "Design Autobiography," *Goldsmiths Journal* 30 (Summer 1980): 28–29.
- Yoshiko Uchida, "Jewelry by Merry Renk," *Craft Horizons*, November/December 1961, 36–37.

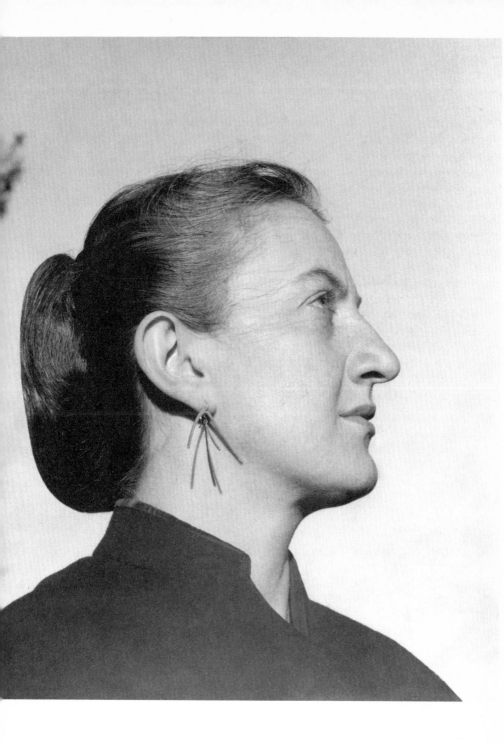

Florence Resnikoff
b. 1920

Jeweler, sculptor, and teacher Florence Resnikoff combined electroforming and anodizing processes with traditional techniques from around the world to yield vibrantly colored, intricately textured jewelry and metalwork. Born in Texas, Resnikoff began exploring jewelry and enameling through adult education courses while working as a registered medical technician in Chicago. In the early 1950s she relocated to Palo Alto, where she had her first single-artist show at Stanford University in 1956. After her second solo show, held at the Chicago Public Library in 1958, she achieved professional-level status in the Metal Arts Guild, a regular gathering of Bay Area metal artists. There she met Margaret De Patta, whose approach to structure and materials guided Resnikoff's investigations, and Bob Winston, who introduced her to wax casting. Her involvement with the guild expanded her repertoire of techniques and materials, and she began to incorporate colorful stones, enamels, and metal casting in her work. In the 1960s Resnikoff advanced her metalwork skills at CCAC (BA, 1967) and San Jose State University (MA, 1973). During this time she learned anodizing and, with the help of a National Endowment for the Arts grant in 1973, studied electroforming with Stanley Lechtzin at the Tyler School of Art in Philadelphia. Both processes were central to her later work, as was bronze casting, which she used in her sculpture and liturgical commissions. In 1973 she returned to CCAC to teach and later became a professor, serving as head of the metal arts program until her retirement in 1989. Among her many honors and numerous exhibitions, Resnikoff was named a Living Treasure of California by the Creative Arts League (1985). ss

Sources
· Hazel Bray, "Florence Resnikoff: Probing the Potential of a New Esthetic," *Metalsmith* 7, no. 4 (Fall 1987): 14–19.
· Study files, Balch Art Research Library, LACMA, DEC.002.

Victor Ries
b. 1907

Best known as an ecclesiastical silversmith, German émigré Victor Ries also made modern secular metal objects and jewelry and was renowned for his elegant and expressive lettering in both English and Hebrew. Ries completed a traditional silversmithing apprenticeship and studied at the Kunstgewerbeschule (School of Fine and Applied Arts) and the Akademie für Freie und Angewandte Kunst (Academy of Fine and Applied Arts) in Berlin before moving to Palestine in 1933, where he opened a metalworking studio and taught briefly at the Bezalel School of Arts and Crafts in Jerusalem. During this time his major commissions included a large-scale map of Israel for a Jerusalem bank, the crest for the city of Haifa, and metalwork for several buildings by architect Erich Mendelsohn. Seeking opportunity in the United States, Ries relocated to San Francisco in 1947, partly at the encouragement of Mendelsohn, who had settled there. Soon thereafter Marguerite Wildenhain invited him to run the metal and jewelry studio at the Pond Farm Workshops, a school and community of craftspeople in Guerneville in Northern California. After the dissolution of the workshops in 1952, Ries set up his own studio in the Bay Area, executing work for synagogues and churches and making ritual objects and jewelry. In the 1970s he moved his workshop to the campus of the Judah L. Magnes Museum, a Jewish museum in Berkeley where he served as artist-in-residence and created the institution's entrance gate at its former location on Russell Street. Ries was closely intertwined in the Northern California craft community as a member of the Designer-Craftsmen of California, the American Craft Council, and the Metal Arts Guild. He exhibited frequently and has been the subject of solo exhibitions at the Jewish Museum in New York (1948) and the M. H. de Young Museum in San Francisco (1954). He taught metalwork throughout his life, with his longest tenure at CCAC from 1953 to 1975. BT

Sources
- Victor Ries, "Religious Artistic Expression in Metal Sculpture," interview by Suzanne B. Riess, 1983, in *Renaissance of Religious Art and Architecture in the San Francisco Bay Area, 1946–1968*, Regional Oral History Office, Bancroft Library, University of California, Berkeley, 1985.
- Study files, Balch Art Research Library, LACMA, DEC.002.

Ed Rossbach
1914–2002

Teacher, author, and fiber art pioneer Ed Rossbach applied his deep knowledge of textile history to a body of work that emphasized expression and experimentation over function, often incorporating unusual materials such as raffia, paper, and cardboard packages, as well as references to popular culture, in his textiles and baskets. Born in Chicago, Rossbach studied painting and design at the University of Washington and art education at Columbia University (MA, 1941). After World War II, he attended the Cranbrook Academy of Art to study ceramics and weaving (MFA, 1947), then returned to the University of Washington to teach textile design. There he met and later married artist Katherine Westphal. The couple moved to Berkeley in 1950 when Rossbach became professor of design at the University of California; he taught there for twenty-nine years. Studying the university's collection of historical textiles informed Rossbach's own exploration of techniques as well as his teaching. Revered for his innovative basketry and use of industrial and ephemeral materials, he treated textiles as an expressive medium and worked in a wide variety of formats (including such off-loom techniques as macramé and plaiting) to explore questions of structure and surface. Awarded a gold medal by the American Craft Council (1990), his work was recognized in several national and international exhibitions, including the Brussels World's Fair (1958) and a retrospective exhibition at the Textile Museum in Washington, D.C. (1990). Rossbach was fascinated by basketry and wrote several seminal books on the subject, including *Baskets as Textile Art* (1973) and *The New Basketry* (1976). JMM

Sources

· Ed Rossbach, interview by Carole Austin, August 27–29, 2002, Archives of American Art, Smithsonian Institution.

· Ed Rossbach and Katherine Westphal, interviews by Paul J. Smith, 1997, Archives of American Art, Smithsonian Institution.

· Paul J. Smith, Jan Janeiro, and Susan Hay, *Ties That Bind: Fiber Art by Ed Rossbach and Katherine Westphal from the Daphne Farago Collection*, exh. cat. (Providence: Museum of Art, Rhode Island School of Design, 1997).

· Ann Pollard Rowe and Rebecca A. T. Stevens, eds., *Ed Rossbach: 40 Years of Exploration and Innovation in Fiber Art*, exh. cat. (Asheville, N.C.: Lark Books; Washington, D.C.: The Textile Museum, 1990).

· Charles Edmund Rossbach, "Artist, Mentor, Professor, Writer," interview by Harriet Nathan, 1983 Regional Oral History Office, Bancroft Library, University of California, Berkeley, 1987.

Hudson Roysher
1911–1993

Silversmith and industrial designer Hudson Roysher readily accepted the necessity of mass production while acknowledging the expressive potential of individually crafted objects, writing: "I want to do my utmost to promote the cause of good individual craftsmanship and design in this machine age."[1] Roysher graduated from the Cleveland School of Art and Western Reserve University in 1934. Five years later he moved to Los Angeles to establish a design department at USC. After serving in World War II, he was the in-house silversmith at Gump's department store in San Francisco but returned to Los Angeles in 1945 to teach industrial design at Chouinard Art Institute. In 1951 Roysher was named professor of art and design at Los Angeles State College, where he taught for twenty-four years. While he designed and patented several objects and tools, including an overhead projector marketed as the *Scribe Visualizer* (1948), he continued his work as a silversmith. He exhibited his hand-raised silver in the May shows at the Cleveland Museum of Art (1932–34, 1936, 1940–41, 1946), in a one-man show at the Los Angeles Museum of History, Science and Art (now LACMA) in 1941, and in many other exhibitions After 1950 Roysher became best known for his ecclesiastical metalwork—candlesticks, chalices, and other religious implements—which adorned numerous Southern California churches. Explaining this shift of focus in his art, he wrote: "I am greatly stimulated by contributing in my small way to the great teachings of the churches."[2] BT

1.
Marguerite Brooks, "Arcadia Professor's Work Helps Cause of Individual Craftsmanship," *Sunday Tribune*, April 6, 1958.
2.
Robert C. Niece, *Art: An Approach* (Dubuque, Iowa: Wm. C. Brown Company Publishers, 1959), 134.

Sources
- Alan Rosenberg, "Hudson Roysher: A Reverence for Silver in the Mid-Twentieth Century," *Silver* 38, no. 3 (May/June 2006): 14–18.
- Myrna Oliver, "Hudson Roysher; Silversmith Created Religious Objects," *Los Angeles Times*, July 9, 1993.
- Janice Lovoos, "Two California Silversmiths," *American Artist* 21, no. 3 (March 1957): 50–52, 62–65.
- "Three Silversmiths," *American Artist* 17, no. 5 (May 1953): 32–34.

As longtime head of the graphics department at Victor Gruen Associates, Marion Sampler used bold environmental graphics to define and animate architectural spaces, declaring that his best work was "anonymous, indivisible, and separable [*sic*] from the hand of the architect."[1] Born in Alabama and raised in Cincinnati, Sampler first studied commercial art but, warned that prospects were dim for African American designers in that field, transferred to USC to pursue a degree in fine arts (BFA, 1955). Sampler was teaching art at Fremont High School when his considerable talents attracted the attention of Saul Bass, who was working with the Urban League and several prominent graphic designers on an initiative to mentor African American and Latino artists in design careers. This connection led Sampler to a position at Victor Gruen Associates (see Victor Gruen) in 1957. He remained with the firm for more than thirty years, serving as head of the graphics department from 1963 and designing everything from environmental signage to company Christmas cards. His designs were vibrant statements of pattern and color, exemplified in graphics programs for several Joseph Magnin specialty stores and a stained-glass dome for the South Coast Plaza shopping center in Costa Mesa. Sampler's reputation for innovative graphics attracted artistic freelance clients as well, including the Craft and Folk Art Museum and the Pacific Design Center in Los Angeles. From the mid-1980s he partnered with designer Anita Berry on architectural graphics for the Beverly Hills Civic Center, among other projects. Sampler won acclaim from the Art Directors Clubs of Los Angeles and New York, and his paintings, drawings, and collages were exhibited at several local galleries. ss

1.
"Marion Sampler," *CA Magazine: Journal of Communication Arts*, 70.

Sources
· *20 Outstanding L.A. Designers*, directed by Archie Boston (1986; Los Angeles: Archie Boston Graphic Design, 2008), DVD.
· "Marion Sampler," *CA Magazine: Journal of Communication Arts* 9, no. 4 (1967): 70–76.
· Study files, Balch Art Research Library, LACMA, DEC.002.

Zahara Schatz
1916–1999

Zahara Schatz combined plastics, metals, and organic materials in her paintings, sculptures, and functional objects, earning special renown for innovations in her signature medium, Plexiglas. Born in Jerusalem, she was the daughter of Boris Schatz, who had founded the Bezalel School of Arts and Crafts in 1906 with the intent of fostering a uniquely Zionist artistic expression. The younger Schatz began her training at Bezalel, followed by study in Paris (1934–37), where she was greatly influenced by European modernism. Arriving in the United States in 1937, she and her brother Bezalel traveled to Jewish organizations, exhibiting both their own art and works by their father and his students. In the early 1940s Schatz settled in Berkeley, where she taught painting at the California Labor School. There she became interested in Plexiglas and experimented with this material alongside sculptor Freda Koblick, who taught plastics courses at the school. Schatz embedded copper wires, metal scraps, and dried leaves into clear resin to create floating abstract compositions, using lamination and heat-forming methods to shape the material into layered paintings and functional objects such as jewelry, serving pieces, and lighting. Her best-known lamp, however, was an enameled steel design that was given an honorable mention in MoMA's 1951 lamp design competition and produced by Heifetz Manufacturing Company. Schatz exhibited regularly in San Francisco and New York, where she kept a studio until 1951, when she returned to Israel to pursue both fine and decorative arts, winning the prestigious Israel Prize on behalf of her family in 1955. Though she maintained a home in Berkeley through the 1970s, she worked primarily in Jerusalem, becoming a successful sculptor. Her monumental aluminum menorah for the Yad Vashem Holocaust memorial (1985) became a symbol of the institution and her most recognized work. ss

Sources
- Gideon Ofrat, *Zahara Schatz, 1916–1999*, exh. cat. (Jerusalem: The Artist's House, 2006).
- Dana Gilerman, "Prof. Schatz's Wayward Children," *Haaretz*, May 1, 2006.
- *The Poet of Light: Zahara Schatz*, directed by Eva Wardi (2004; Helsinki), film.
- Margaret Anderson, "An Artist Works in Plastic," *Craft Horizons*, July/August 1952, 8–12.

233

Lanette Scheeline
1910–2001

Known for her vivid, stylized wallpaper and textile designs, Lanette Scheeline's custom and production work was often inspired by the vistas and landscape of her native Bay Area. Scheeline graduated from the College of Fine Arts at the University of California, Berkeley, in 1932. After one year of teaching high school, she turned to designing window displays and briefly attended the Rudolph Schaeffer School of Design in San Francisco. Her career in textiles began in the 1930s when she started cutting stencils and air-brushing her designs at home. She moved on to cutting wood and linoleum blocks to produce special-order textiles. One of her earliest designs—a marine view of the new Golden Gate Bridge with seagulls—was featured on the cover of the November 1936 issue of *Sunset* magazine and resulted in new clients and praise from decorators. Early recognition also came with the exhibition of three hand-printed textiles at the Golden Gate International Exposition (1939–40), and her fabrics were soon displayed at the upscale home decor retailer W. & J. Sloane in San Francisco. She gained additional experience in the industry while working for Louma Hand Prints, a textile screenprinting factory in San Francisco. Common design motifs throughout her career included local and exotic flora and fauna as well as scenes of natural and built landscapes. In the early 1960s Scheeline moved to New York City, where she worked as a designer for commercial firms, including wallpaper company Katzenbach & Warren. JMM

Sources
· Lanette Scheeline Collection, 1945–1970, Cooper-Hewitt Museum Archives, Smithsonian Institution.
· Janet Robb Cohen-Faure, "Patterns from California Scenery Identify Work of San Francisco Designer," *Christian Science Monitor*, August 20, 1952.

Lanette Scheeline, *Egyptian Garden* textile, c. 1939. Gift of Lanette Scheeline, Smithsonian Institution, Cooper-Hewitt, National Design Museum.

June Schwarcz
b. 1918

Enamel artist June Schwarcz creates tactile, expressive objects by applying technical mastery of her medium to vessel forms and plaques, which she considers nonfunctional sculpture. Born in Denver, Schwarcz (née June Morris) studied industrial design at Pratt Institute in New York from 1939 to 1941 and afterward created packages, greeting cards, textiles, and window displays in New York. In 1943 she married Leroy Schwarcz, an engineer whose work necessitated several moves. While visiting Denver en route to Sausalito in 1954, Schwarcz was introduced to enameling. She began creating enamels with pre-made metal forms but soon began pounding out her own, developing an expertise in the basse-taille technique. When she moved to New Haven, Connecticut, in 1955, Schwarcz traveled to New York City to see examples of contemporary enamel. The curator of the Museum of Contemporary Crafts included her work in the museum's inaugural exhibition, *Craftsmanship in a Changing World* (1956), establishing her reputation. When Schwarcz moved to La Jolla later that year, she showed with the Allied Craftsmen of San Diego and received her first solo exhibition at the La Jolla Art Center (1957). That same year she returned to Sausalito. Beginning in 1962, Schwarcz used electroplating and electroforming to create more dramatic textures and varied shapes. Her innovative use of copper foil and mesh, which she started using in 1964, enables her to fold, cut, gather, and stitch to create unique, dynamic forms. Designated a Living Treasure of California in 1985, Schwarcz also received the James Renwick Alliance Masters of the Medium Award (2009). Since the late 1950s her work has appeared in numerous exhibitions and has been the subject of solo shows at the San Francisco Craft and Folk Art Museum (1998) and the Mingei International Museum in San Diego (2009–10). JMM

Sources
· June Schwarcz Papers, [c. 1960–]2000, Archives of American Art, Smithsonian Institution.
· June Schwarcz, interview by Arline M. Fisch, January 21, 2001, Archives of American Art, Smithsonian Institution.
· Carole Austin, *June Schwarcz: Forty Years/Forty Pieces*, exh. cat. (San Francisco: San Francisco Craft & Folk Art Museum, 1998).

Kay Sekimachi
b. 1926

Kay Sekimachi is a master of both traditional weaving techniques and experimental fiber constructions, exploring materials and structures that take her work beyond cloth to three-dimensional sculpture. Born in San Francisco to Japanese immigrant parents, Sekimachi and her family were sent to internment camps during World War II. When she returned to her home in Berkeley, she studied design briefly at CCAC. In 1949 she discovered weaving and left college to pursue her craft through night school and an apprenticeship. Sekimachi returned to CCAC to take summer courses with Trude Guermonprez, who steered her toward more experimental weaving techniques and complex structures such as double-weaves. Though she worked mainly for exhibition in galleries and museums, Sekimachi developed some production designs, most notably for Jack Lenor Larsen, her instructor at the Haystack Mountain School of Crafts in Maine and one of her staunchest supporters. Over time Sekimachi's art became increasingly less functional. Experiments with double-weaves led her to work in multiple layers, and in 1963 she began a series of three-dimensional hangings made from nylon monofilament. While her early textiles appeared in several major crafts exhibitions, including *Designer-Craftsmen USA* (1953), these new pieces became associated with the emerging field of fiber art and were included in landmark shows such as MoMA's *Wall Hangings* (1969) and *Deliberate Entanglements* at UCLA (1971). In 1972 Sekimachi married wood turner Bob Stocksdale. In her recent work, she continues to experiment with new forms and fibers, creating boxes, baskets, jewelry, and other objects. ss

Sources
· Bob Stocksdale and Kay Sekimachi Papers, 1937–2004, Archives of American Art, Smithsonian Institution.
· Kay Sekimachi [Stocksdale], interview by Suzanne Baizerman, July 26–August 6, 2001, Archives of American Art, Smithsonian Institution.
· Kay Sekimachi, "The Weaver's Weaver: Explorations in Multiple Layers and Three-Dimensional Fiber Art," interview by Harriet Nathan, 1993, Regional Oral History Office, Bancroft Library, University of California, Berkeley, 1996.
· Signe Mayfield, *Marriage in Form: Kay Sekimachi and Bob Stocksdale* (Palo Alto: Palo Alto Cultural Center, 1993).
· Yoshiko Uchida, "Kay Sekimachi," *Craft Horizons*, May/June 1959, 21–23.

Millard Sheets
1907–1989

One of the most prominent figures in the Southern California art and design community, Millard Sheets exerted a wide influence through his prolific artistic practice, his role as an educator, and his curatorial initiatives. A Pomona native, Sheets studied art and taught watercolor at Chouinard Art Institute, where his virtuosic and innovative use of the medium and focus on California subject matter established his reputation. Upon graduation in 1929, he was represented by the influential Dalzell Hatfield Galleries in Los Angeles. In accordance with his belief that art should be integral to all aspects of daily living, Sheets also worked in the applied arts. From 1931 to 1953 he designed and painted murals for public and private buildings, created department store displays, and produced illustrations. This business evolved into his Claremont-based firm Millard Sheets Design, Inc., which designed and executed large-scale murals, mosaics, and stained-glass windows. Sheets's artistic legacy in Southern California is most visible in the design and decoration of more than 120 branches of the Home Savings and Loan Association, an endeavor he began in 1952. His influence was also felt through his teaching and curatorial efforts. He served on the faculty and later as director of art at Scripps College and Claremont Graduate School, where he hired both William Manker and Richard B. Petterson, and was director of the Los Angeles County Art Institute, where he appointed Peter Voulkos to teach ceramics (though he later condemned Voulkos's unorthodox behavior and work). As director of art exhibitions at the Los Angeles County Fair from 1931 to 1956, Sheets exposed the work of contemporary local artists and craftspeople to a broad public. He was also responsible, with Petterson, for several important craft and design exhibitions at the fair, including *6000 Years: Art in Clay* (1952), a universal history of ceramics; *The Arts of Daily Living* (1954), a show organized in collaboration with Elizabeth Gordon, editor of *House Beautiful*, which featured twenty-two model room settings that demonstrated an organic form of modernism; and *The Arts of Western Living* (1955), a follow-up to the previous year's exhibition that focused on the craft and design produced in the region. In the 1970s Sheets built a home and studio, which he called Barking Rocks, in Gualala in Mendocino County on California's coast, settling there permanently in 1978. JMM

Sources
· Millard Sheets Papers, 1907–1990, Archives of American Art, Smithsonian Institution.
· Gordon T. McClelland, *Millard Sheets: The Early Years (1926–1944)* (Newport Beach: California Regionalist Art Information Center, 2010).
· Millard Sheets, interview by Paul Karlstrom, October 1986–July 1988, Archives of American Art, Smithsonian Institution.
· Millard Sheets, "Los Angeles Art Community: Group Portrait," interview by George M. Goodwin, 1977, Oral History Program of the University of California Los Angeles.
· Arthur Millier, Hartley Burr Alexander, and Merle Armitage, *Millard Sheets* (Los Angeles: Dalzell Hatfield, 1935).

Otis Shepard
1893–1969

Best known for his stylized and airbrushed posters, art director Otis Shepard incorporate modern design elements into his billboard graphics and branding schemes. Originally from Kansas, Shepard left his transient Midwestern family for Oakland around 1905. The cartoons he drew as an apprentice in the *San Francisco Chronicle* art department attracted the attention of the city's leading outdoor advertising firm, Foster & Kleiser, which hired him in 1917. He became the firm's art director in 1923 and established his reputation with a series of national advertising campaigns. Though he tailored his illustrative style to fit each project, Shepard advocated a modern approach to American advertising, promoting the use of symbolic imagery and branding through repetition. In 1929 he moved to New York to start a freelance practice, creating poster designs for clients such as Chesterfield Cigarettes and Chevrolet. He was named art director for the Wrigley Company of Chicago in 1932 and oversaw not only advertising but also designs for other company interests, which included the Chicago Cubs. In the 1930s he spent several years on Wrigley-owned Catalina Island, collaborating with wife Dorothy Shepard (1906–2000) to recast the resort as a romantic vestige of Alta California in an ambitious project that encompassed everything from city planning and street lamps to matchbook design. By contrast, the reductivist imagery and expert airbrushing he used on Wrigley's widely acclaimed posters demonstrated his awareness of European modernism, especially the work of Austrian émigré Joseph Binder. After thirty-one years at Wrigley, Shepard retired to Belvedere, near San Francisco. ss

Sources
- Steve Strauss, *Moving Images: The Transportation Poster in America* (New York: Fullcourt Press, 1984).
- Augusta Leinard, "Otis Shepard: Man and Artist," *The Poster: National Journal of Outdoor Advertising and Poster Art*, July 1929, 16–19.

Otis Shepard (right) and wife Dorothy.

Julius Shulman
1910–2009

Julius Shulman's iconic images of modern architecture defined the ideal of glamorous yet relaxed mid-century living. Shulman, a Brooklyn native, moved with his family to Los Angeles in 1920. From 1929 to 1935 he audited classes, first at UCLA and later at the University of California, Berkeley. Though his only formal training was through a high school photography class, at Berkeley he began selling photographs he had taken for pleasure. Returning to Los Angeles in 1936, he paid a visit to Richard Neutra's Kun House, then under construction. Neutra happened to see Shulman's photographs of the building, bought the images, hired Shulman for additional projects, and introduced him to other important architects in Los Angeles. Along with his architectural commissions, Shulman took product photographs and advertising portraits and began accepting assignments for *Arts and Architecture* magazine in 1938. From 1943 to 1945 he served as a photographer at a U.S. Army hospital in Spokane, Washington, resuming his career in Los Angeles after the war. In 1950 he moved into a home and studio in Laurel Canyon designed by friend and client Raphael Soriano and hired a small staff, including an in-house printer. From the late 1940s into the late 1960s he took on assignments for popular and shelter magazines, expanding his client list beyond Los Angeles. His images, which were highly staged and often included people to give a sense of scale and human interest, captured the aspirational modern lifestyle and remain powerful representations of the era. Vocal in his dislike of postmodern architecture, Shulman retired in 1986, only to reemerge in 2000 at age ninety with German photographer Juergen Nogai as collaborator. Shulman's legacy as an architectural photographer and purveyor of modernism is ensured by numerous publications celebrating his photographs and the image of modern living he helped craft. JMM

Sources
- Julius Shulman Photography Archive, Getty Research Institute, Los Angeles.
- *Visual Acoustics: The Modernism of Julius Shulman*, directed by Eric Bricker (2008; New York: Arthouse Films, distributed by New Video, 2010), DVD.
- Julius Shulman, *Julius Shulman: Architecture and Its Photography*, ed. Peter Gössel (Cologne: Taschen, 1998).
- Joseph Rosa, *A Constructed View: The Architectural Photography of Julius Shulman* (New York: Rizzoli, 1994).
- Julius Shulman, interview by Taina Rikala De Noriega, January 12–February 3, 1990, Archives of American Art, Smithsonian Institution.

Julius Shulman at the Stahl House (Case Study House #22), Los Angeles, 1960.

Graphic designer Nicolas Sidjakov developed an expressive illustration style that incorporated historic imagery and reflected childhood wonder, exemplifying the eclecticism that flourished in graphic design during the 1960s and 1970s. Born in Latvia, Sidjakov studied painting at the École des Beaux-Arts (School of Fine Arts) in Paris but was unsatisfied with this traditional training. Instead, he began working for Parisian design studios, developing promotional materials for French cinema. In 1956 he married Jean McFarland, an American, and the couple moved to the Bay Area, eventually settling in Sausalito. After a brief stint with Design Corporation of America, Sidjakov opened his own firm in San Francisco and designed advertisements and graphics for such clients as Bank of America, Youngstown Steel, and Eichler Homes. In 1961 he won the prestigious Caldecott Medal for *Baboushka and the Three Kings* (1960), one of several children's books he illustrated for Parnassus Press. For the book's illustrations, Sidjakov emulated the look of traditional Russian woodcuts by drawing on rice paper coated with rubber cement, an inventive use of materials and techniques. His design work was widely celebrated, appearing frequently in *Communication Arts* and *Print* as well as in major art directors' shows. In 1978 he partnered with graphic designer Jerry Berman to form Sidjakov & Berman (later Sidjakov, Berman & Gomez), a consultant graphic design firm known for its witty and imaginative packages, advertisements, and corporate graphics. ss

Sources
· Valerie F. Brooks, "Sensibly in All Directions," *Print*, May/June 1981, 44–53.
· "Nicolas Sidjakov," *Communication Arts* 12, no. 3 (1970): 42–49.
· "Nicolas Sidjakov," *CA (Communication Arts)*, June 1962, 32–35.
· Ruth Robbins, "Nicolas Sidjakov," *The Horn Book Magazine*, August 1961, 323–26.

A founding father of American industrial design, Joseph Sinel advocated a machine aesthetic and actively promoted the importance of industrial designers in modern society. Born in New Zealand, Sinel was a commercial artist before coming to San Francisco in 1918. He worked for several notable advertising firms, including Foster & Kleiser, before opening his own office. His commissions expanded to include product designs by 1921, a date he used to support his claim that he was the first established industrial designer in the United States. Working in New York from 1923 to 1936 before returning permanently to California, he designed products with clean lines and minimal ornamentation for clients such as International Ticket Scale, Remington, and Toastmaster. Equally adept at graphic design, he developed over three hundred trademarks and designed books for commercial firms such as Random House and for private presses such as San Francisco's Grabhorn Press. His *Book of American Trade-marks & Devices* (1924) emphasized the need for simple, professional trademarks, challenging designers to elevate what Sinel saw as the reigning vulgarity of popular taste. In 1944 he joined with fourteen industry leaders to form the Society of Industrial Designers, an organization that helped define this new profession. Though his office was in San Francisco, he lectured and taught at schools throughout California as well as at Pratt Institute in New York. Sinel's most enduring relationship, however, was with CCAC, where he taught in the 1920s and in 1949–50, and which awarded him an honorary doctorate (1958) and commemorated his career with an exhibition in 1970. ss

Sources
· Joseph C. Sinel Collection, Simpson Library,
 California College of the Arts, San Francisco.
· Arthur J. Pulos, "Joseph Claude Sinel, 1889–1975,"
 Industrial Design, May 1975, 8.
· "Jo Sinel's Super Show," *CCAC Review*, Autumn
 1970, 10–11.
· Dorothy Wagner Puccinelli, "Joseph Sinel, Industrial
 Designer," *Arts and Architecture*, June 1941, 23.

Don Smith
1918–1972

San Francisco designer Don Smith combined bright colors and whimsical, Cubist-inspired forms in his interior and product designs. Born in Salinas, Smith studied drawing and design at Salinas Junior College and later at Chouinard Art Institute and the Rudolph Schaeffer School of Design. During World War II he served as a photographer in the U.S. Navy. While working as display director for Gump's department store in San Francisco from 1946 to 1949, Smith earned a reputation for his window displays and colorful shopping-bag designs. In the 1950s he worked as a freelance designer and art director on various exhibitions, commercial interior displays, logos, wallpaper, fabrics, and printed materials, and from about 1954 to 1959 he partnered with Gene Tepper in the firm Smith/Tepper Design (known c. 1956–58 as Smith, Tepper and Sundberg). Clients included prominent Bay Area businesses as well as national and international companies such as Japan Airlines. Smith also taught at several Bay Area arts institutions. In 1959 he moved to Chicago to become director of graphics at the design firm Latham Tyler Jensen. Returning to San Francisco in 1961, he worked as a freelance designer until his death. Smith's advertising art was highly regarded in the field, and his designs were featured in national exhibitions, including his *Windmobile* wallpaper, which appeared in *Design in the Kitchen* (1949) at the San Francisco Museum of Art (now SFMOMA) and won the Annual International Design Competition from the American Institute of Decorators the same year, and his *Hopscotch* textile, which was shown in *Good Design* at the Chicago Merchandise Mart (1951). JMM

Sources
· Study files, Balch Art Research Library, LACMA, DEC.002.

b. 1920

Printer Jack Werner Stauffacher blends classical and experimental typographical approaches to elucidate texts and recontextualize historic letterforms. For more than forty years he has engaged in experiments that juxtapose letters of varying sizes, shapes, and orientations to produce nonlinear abstractions and force viewers to reconsider their assumptions about type. The best-known example of this work is the cover of overlapping letters for the *Journal of Typographic Research*, which was introduced in 1967 and used for many years thereafter. Stauffacher grew up in San Mateo, where he began printing at age fourteen. In 1936 he founded the Greenwood Press in a studio behind his family's home. Though largely self-taught, Stauffacher was inspired by the writings of typographers Daniel Updike and Jan Tschichold. After serving as a topographer in World War II, he returned to the Bay Area, where he collaborated with avant-garde artists, including his brother, cinematographer Frank Stauffacher. Building on his acclaimed study *Janson: A Definitive Collection* (1954), Stauffacher was awarded a Fulbright scholarship to Italy in 1955 to study the history of the Florentine book. He began teaching at the Carnegie Institute of Technology in Pittsburgh in 1958, where he reestablished Porter Garnett's Laboratory Press before returning to California in 1963 to direct the Stanford University Press. In 1966 he relaunched the Greenwood Press in San Francisco. His scholarly pursuit of clarifying complex texts through thoughtful design culminated in the radical 1978 edition of Plato's *Phaedrus*. Over the years he has remained committed to Janson type, publishing a book about the typeface's creator titled *Nicholas Kis: A Hungarian Punch-Cutter and Printer, 1650–1702* (1983) and advising on the digitized versions of the typeface. ss

Sources
- Jack Werner Stauffacher, *A Typographic Journey: The History of the Greenwood Press and Bibliography, 1934–2000* (San Francisco: Book Club of California, 1999).
- Chuck Byrne, "Jack Stauffacher, Printer &c," *Émigré*, Winter 1998, 17–28.
- Jack Werner Stauffacher, "A Printed Word Has Its Own Measure," interview by Ruth Teiser, 1969, Regional Oral History Office, Bancroft Library, University of California, Berkeley.

Bob Stocksdale
1913–2003

Among the leading figures in the postwar wood-turning movement and often credited with elevating the craft to art, Bob Stocksdale reveled in the grain of his exotic woods, using them to create visual poetry out of functional forms. Stocksdale was raised on a farm outside of Huntington, Indiana, where he set up his first woodworking shop. Prior to World War II he honed his largely self-taught woodworking skills through various jobs. While confined at a conscientious objector camp in Valhalla, Michigan, during the war, he started making bowls and plates that he sold through the Columbus, Ohio, craft shop of Helen Winnemore, an ardent Quaker who supported both his pacifist beliefs and his work. After he was moved to a camp east of San Francisco, Gump's department store started selling his turned wares. Following his release in 1946, he established his workshop in Berkeley. Stocksdale began using rare exotic woods to craft bowls that, though still utilitarian in form, were acclaimed for their attractive grain patterns, and he sold these works through Fraser's, a gallery and furniture shop in Berkeley. A member of the International Wood Collectors Society, he emphasized the unusual grains and patterns in his material as he shaped elegant, thin-walled, and deceptively simple forms. In 1972 Stocksdale married fiber artist Kay Sekimachi. He displayed work in international traveling exhibitions organized by the U.S. State Department and the Brussels World's Fair (1958), as well as local and national shows, including *California Design* and MoMA's *Good Design*. Awarded a gold medal by the American Craft Council (1995), he has been the subject of several single-artist exhibitions, including shows at the Long Beach Museum of Art (1959), the Museum of Contemporary Crafts in New York (1965), and the San Francisco Museum of Craft and Folk Art (2001). JMM

Sources
· Bob Stocksdale and Kay Sekimachi Papers, 1937–2004, Archives of American Art, Smithsonian Institution.
· Ron Roszkiewicz, *To Turn the Perfect Wooden Bowl: The Lifelong Quest of Bob Stocksdale* (East Petersburg, Pa.: Fox Chapel, 2009).
· Bob Stocksdale, interview by Signe Mayfield, February 16–March 21, 2001, Archives of American Art, Smithsonian Institution.
· Carolyn Kastner, ed., *Bob Stocksdale: Eighty-Eight Turnings*, exh. cat. (San Francisco: Museum of Craft and Folk Art, 2001).

· Bob Stocksdale, "Pioneer Wood-Lathe Artist, and Master Creator of Bowls from Fine and Rare Woods," interview by Harriet Nathan, 1996, Regional Oral History Office, Bancroft Library, University of California, Berkeley, 1998.

Martin Streich
1926–1999

Oakland craftsman Martin Streich used metal-raising and casting techniques to make contemporary jewelry characterized by abstract shapes and biomorphic forms. Streich attended San Francisco State University (BA, 1958) and took courses at several Bay Area art institutions, including CCAC and the Rudolph Schaeffer School of Design. An accomplished craftsman and draftsman—he worked as a cabinetmaker and architectural model maker early in his career—Streich took summer courses with Margaret De Patta, which crystallized his interest in jewelry. De Patta's emphasis on abstract geometric forms and relatively inexpensive materials such as sterling silver, copper, brass, and wood was reflected in Streich's work. From 1951 to 1963 he created custom and limited-production pieces sold through the San Francisco modern jewelry shop Nanny's, as well as Gump's department store. Streich joined the metalwork and jewelry faculty at CCAC in 1959. During his forty-year tenure, he held many administrative roles and established CCAC's Mexican studies program in El Molino, Mexico. BT

Sources
- "California College of Arts and Crafts," *Creative Crafts*, July/August 1961, 10–14.
- Study files, Balch Art Research Library, LACMA, DEC.002.

Martin Streich (left) and CCAC students.

Elza Sunderland
1903–1991

Elza of Hollywood, the flamboyantly named business founded in 1937 by Elza Sunderland in downtown Los Angeles, produced thousands of striking designs for both clothing and furnishing textiles. Inspired by the landscape and culture of California as well as of Mexico and the South Pacific, she capitalized on the contemporary taste for vivid color and intense patterns. Her most popular design was a strawberry motif that was reputedly produced in a run of more than 250,000 yards. Noting her bold use of color, the fashion trade journal *California Stylist* identified "Color-fornia" as Elza of Hollywood's trade slogan in 1939. Born Elza Wilheim in Hungary, Sunderland immigrated with her family to New York City in 1910, where she studied design and textiles at Washington Irving High School, a girls' technical school at the time. In 1937 she moved west to Los Angeles with her husband, Don Sunderland, and established Elza of Hollywood to design and produce fashion and furnishing textiles. By 1938 Bullock's department store was marketing her Tropi-Cal Fabrics, and she had become so associated with Southern California that the advertisements touted her as "an artist of Los Angeles." She created printed fabrics for many leaders of the California fashion industry, including swimwear and sportswear designers Mary Ann DeWeese and Rose Marie Reid, as well as manufacturers Cole of California and Catalina Sportwear. JMM

Sources
· Elza Sunderland Textile Design Collection, LACMA.
· Betty Goodwin, "Elza Sunderland, a Pioneer in Textile Design," *Los Angeles Times*, June 6, 1986.
· June Lee Smith, "Reversal Spurred Success for California Designer of Dramatic Textiles," *Christian Science Monitor*, May 21, 1948.

ELZA OF HOLLYWOOD

Deborah Sussman
b. 1931

Internationally acclaimed graphic and environmental designer Deborah Sussman applies her expertise in color and branding to interiors, buildings, and even entire cities. Educated at Bard College, Black Mountain College, and the Institute of Design in Chicago, the native New Yorker came to Los Angeles in 1953 to intern at the Eames Office (see Charles and Ray Eames). For four years Sussman worked on toys, packaging, graphics, exhibitions, and films. She would later credit her predilection for color and folk art to these formative years with Ray Eames and designer Alexander Girard, a frequent visitor and sometime collaborator at the Eames Office. In 1957 Sussman was awarded a Fulbright fellowship to study at the Hochschule für Gestaltung (School of Design) in Ulm, Germany. She returned to the Eames Office in 1960 but also established an independent practice, creating branding and interiors for several Los Angeles retailers. In 1968 she founded Deborah Sussman & Company, which became Sussman/Prejza in 1980, when she partnered with her husband, architect Paul Prejza (b. 1939). The firm's prominent client list included Apple Inc., Hasbro, Walt Disney World, and the cities of Philadelphia, Santa Monica, and Culver City. Sussman/Prejza collaborated with the Jerde Partnership on an inventive kit of parts for the 1984 Los Angeles Olympics. Applied on temporary architecture, the design unified multiple locations with signature graphics and a vibrant palette reflecting the influence of Pacific Rim cultures. Among her many honors, Sussman was awarded a doctorate of humane letters from Bard College (1998) and an AIGA medal (2004) and is an elected member of the Alliance Graphique Internationale. Her work was exhibited in the School of Visual Arts' Masters Series (1995). ss

Sources
- Joseph Giovannini, "Turning Surface into Symbol," *Architectural Record*, January 2006, 74–78.
- Sussman/Prejza & Company, *Beyond Graphic Design: Sussman/Prejza & Company* (Tokyo: Process Architecture, 1995).
- Dugald Stermer, "Deborah Sussman," *Communication Arts*, January/February 1985, 28–39.

La Gardo Tackett
1911–1984

After an early career as a craftsman-potter, La Gardo Tackett turned to designing mass-produced ceramics for the home and garden, enlivening his smooth surfaces and simple forms with bursts of color and whimsical cartoons. Born in Kentucky, Tackett studied art and geology at Indiana University, a combination that led to his interest in clay. He worked as an art director in New York City and then moved to Los Angeles in the early 1940s with his wife, Virginia Roth Tackett (1913–1982), who later served as his business manager. In the early years Tackett made ceramics by hand, often in irregular shapes and with animal motifs. He entered Claremont Graduate School in 1949 and studied ceramics with Richard B. Petterson, but ultimately disavowed the prevailing influence of Chinese and Japanese ceramics, instead pursuing "objective forms" characterized by neutral color and simple shapes inspired by Classical Greek pottery and Dutch and Russian Constructivists, including Piet Mondrian, Theo van Doesburg, and Naum Gabo. He was also an instructor at the short-lived California School of Art in Los Angeles. In one project, he asked students to create modern planter designs using molds from traditional terracotta pots. The result eventually became the first line produced by Architectural Pottery in 1950, and Tackett himself subsequently designed for the company. After a brief partnership with Kenji Fujita to make ceramic housewares, Tackett moved to Japan in the late 1950s, where he supervised production of his porcelain dinnerware for Schmid Kreglinger of Boston. He returned to the United States in about 1962 and settled in Connecticut. Both his early and later works were widely exhibited—his early handmade pieces were shown in the U.S. State Department's international traveling exhibition *Design for Use, USA* (1951–53), and the later production designs appeared in the *Good Design* and *California Design* exhibitions. ss

Sources
- La Gardo Tackett Papers, Museum of California Design, Los Angeles.
- La Gardo Tackett, "A New Causal Structure for Ceramic Design," *Arts and Architecture*, April 1955, 14–15, 30.
- Gertrude Roher, "The Potter of Topanga Canyon," *Craft Horizons*, Autumn 1949, 20–22.

Gene Tepper
b. 1919

A self-taught industrial designer, Gene Tepper created products, graphics, and furniture that emphasized human engineering and efficiency factors over superfluous styling. Originally from Washington, D.C., Tepper attended classes at the Art Students League and the New School for Social Research in New York (1937–40) and began his career as a display and exhibition designer. He settled in San Francisco in 1948, initially working for Walter Landor before establishing Gene Tepper Associates in 1951. From about 1954 to 1959 he partnered with Don Smith (Smith/Tepper Design; known c. 1956–58 as Smith, Tepper and Sundberg) and from 1965 to 1973, with Budd Steinhilber (Tepper & Steinhilber Associates, Inc.). Working in the heart of California's burgeoning high-tech industry, Tepper built a large client base of technology and industrial firms—including Lockheed, Standard Oil, Hewlett-Packard, and IBM—for which he developed electronics, medical instrumentation, measurement and testing equipment, and other products. Tepper also created home furnishings, earning special renown for an iron fireplace set and a convertible coffee table/dining table known as the *Versitable*. The latter was included in the Chicago Merchandise Mart and MoMA's 1951 *Good Design* exhibition. When shown in Chicago, it was ranked first by retail store buyers for its affordability and practical design. His work was featured in the first *California Design* exhibition (1954–55) and in *California Design 11* (1971), and he taught industrial design at San Jose State University, the California School of Fine Arts, and the Rudolph Schaeffer School of Design. LS

Sources
· J.R.M. (probably Judith Ransom Miller), "Gene Tepper Associates, Inc.," *Industrial Design*, June 1966, 106–7.
· Study files, Balch Art Research Library, LACMA, DEC.002.

Dorothy C. Thorpe
1901–1989

A designer of tableware, glassware, ceramics, and linens, Dorothy C. Thorpe achieved international renown with simple, elegant designs—particularly in glass—in a career that spanned more than four decades. A native of Salt Lake City, Thorpe studied at Latter-Day Saints' University and the University of Utah. By 1926 she had moved to California and settled in Glendale. With no training in design, she began to decorate glassware in 1931. Among her first works were tumblers made from beer bottles (though some sources claim they were wine bottles) adorned with what Thorpe, in a letter from 1945, called "lovely colors of raffia to go with California pottery for dinner in the patio."[1] Her sand-blasted glass with floral motifs, introduced in the 1930s, and her silver-rimmed cocktail ware, introduced in the 1950s, sparked national trends. Thorpe first sold her products through a Hollywood gift shop until high-end retailers took note. When it opened in 1939, the May Company department store on Wilshire Boulevard in Los Angeles featured the Dorothy Thorpe Shop, and Dorothy C. Thorpe Originals became a distinctive California brand carried by department stores across the country, including Gump's, Gimbels, Marshall Field's, and Bloomingdale's. Thorpe's designs were executed at her factory in Glendale until 1963, by which time she had sold her controlling interest in the company following the death of her husband, who was also her business partner. The company subsequently moved to Sun Valley in California's northern San Fernando Valley. Many of Thorpe's designs, such as her dinnerware line with ball handles for New Zealand's Crown Lynn Potteries, were manufactured by international companies. Her work was widely exhibited, including at the Golden Gate International Exposition (1939–40) and in *Useful Objects in Wartime* (MoMA, 1942). JMM

1.
Dorothy Thorpe to J. Stanley Brothers Jr., October 22, 1945. Dorothy Thorpe study file, Balch Art Research Library, LACMA.

Sources
- Dorothy C. Thorpe Biography File, Special Collections, Glendale Public Library, Glendale, Calif.
- Valerie Ringer Monk, *Crown Lynn: A New Zealand Icon* (Auckland: Penguin, 2006), 86–89.
- Sam Bagby, "An Old Bottle Launched a Career," *Los Angeles Times Home* magazine, November 2, 1941.
- Study files, Balch Art Research Library, LACMA, DEC.002.

Adolph Tischler
b. 1917

Flatware designer Adolph Tischler belongs to the generation of World War II veterans who, seeking to establish careers in the postwar era, turned to arts and crafts training to learn the necessary skills. Born in Atlantic City, New Jersey, Tischler studied briefly at the Kann Institute of Art in Los Angeles, which accepted many returning GIs. He subsequently owned and operated a small factory that produced jewelry and metal products. Primarily self-taught in metalworking, Tischler designed several handmade and production lines of silver and stainless-steel flatware that were distributed through department and specialty stores such as Van Keppel-Green and I. Magnin. Functionality and comfort were primary concerns, and his ergonomic forms were designed to fit easily in the hand. He was also interested in exploiting new materials, as seen in his *Duo* flatware pattern, for which he used injection-molded nylon to emulate more costly ebony. Tischler had several ties to the Los Angeles design community, as he commissioned a house from architect R. M. Schindler in Westwood (1949–50), and his flatware was owned by Julius Shulman. Tischler's professional work as a flatware designer ended when he embarked on a new career as a graphic designer for the Aerospace Corporation around 1960, although he continued to make metal objects for personal use throughout his life. BT

Sources
· Study files, Balch Art Research Library, LACMA, DEC.002.

Adolph Tischler, *Duo* flatware, c. 1955.
LACMA, Purchased with funds provided by Harris & Ruble.

Nathan Turk produced well-tailored, brightly hued clothing favored by Western enter-tainers and movie stars and known for its extensive embellishment with embroidery and fringe. Born Note Teig in a village near Minsk in what was then Russia (now Belarus), Turk apprenticed at a young age to a tailor in Warsaw. He immigrated to the United States in 1913 and adopted the surname Turk, settling first in New York and then in Los Angeles, where he built a shop in 1923 in what was then a rural part of the San Fernando Valley (now Sherman Oaks). First named Turk's Riding Apparel, the store was later called Turk's English and Western Apparel Shop. Republic Studios, producer of countless Western films, was founded in nearby Studio City in 1935, and by the late 1930s Turk's shop was frequently patronized by celluloid cowboys like Gene Autry and Roy Rogers. He attracted a following among musicians and movie stars with a colorful look that combined meticulous tailoring with Western design details such as embroidered patterns inspired by European peasant traditions and Mexican and Native American motifs. The popularity of dude ranches boosted his business, and Turk's clothing was sold through high-end department stores as well as in his shop. After World War II, he opened a small factory in Hollywood, but this venture was short-lived. Turk retired in the mid-1970s and sold his equipment and materials to Manuel Cuevas, another celebrated Western-wear tailor. JMM

Sources
· Peter La Chapelle, *Proud to Be an Okie: Cultural Politics, Country Music, and Migration in Southern California* (Berkeley: University of California Press, 2007), 152–54, 291–92.
· Tyler Beard and Jim Arndt, *100 Years of Western Wear*, rev. ed. (Layton, Utah: Gibbs Smith, 2001).
· Holly George-Warren and Michelle Freedman, *How the West Was Worn* (New York: Abrams; Los Angeles: Autry Museum of Western Heritage, 2001).

Paul Tuttle
1918–2002

Furniture designer Paul Tuttle explored the limits of materials and constantly revisited his own forms, some of which he perfected over decades. The Missouri-born designer attended Art Center School on the GI Bill but was expelled by Alvin Lustig for his lack of drafting skills. Lustig, nevertheless, was impressed by Tuttle's creativity and hired him as a studio assistant. After studying with Frank Lloyd Wright at Taliesin West in Scottsdale, Arizona (1948–49), Tuttle returned to Los Angeles, where he worked as an interior designer in the architecture firms of Welton Becket and Thornton Ladd. During the early 1950s he handcrafted wood furniture in a Scandinavian-influenced style but soon began designing for production. In 1956 he moved to Santa Barbara, and, in addition to his furniture career, he executed six architectural projects, one of which was his own home. From 1958 to 1983 Tuttle lived part-time in Switzerland, where he designed luxurious leather and steel furniture for Strässle International. His furniture won the admiration of curator Eudorah Moore, who selected several pieces for the *California Design* exhibitions before organizing Tuttle's first retrospective at the Pasadena Art Museum (1966). Beginning in 1981, he collaborated with Santa Barbara–area craftsmen Stanley Reifel, Bud Tullis, and Jeff Walker on custom pieces for private clients. A National Endowment for the Arts grant (1982) allowed him the luxury of designing without a client and led to a series of radical furniture designs exhibited at the University Art Museum, University of California, Santa Barbara (1987). His later furniture reflected a postmodern sensibility, often incorporating ironic references to historical sources and vernacular objects such as cattle harnesses and automobiles. ss

Sources
- Paul Tuttle Collection, Architecture and Design Collection, Art, Design & Architecture Museum, University of California, Santa Barbara.
- Marla Berns, *Paul Tuttle Designs*, exh. cat. (Santa Barbara: University Art Museum, University of California, 2003).
- *Paul Tuttle: Design + the 80s*, exh. cat., essays by David Gebhard and Phyllis Plous (Santa Barbara: University Art Museum, University of California, 1987).
- Eudorah M. Moore, *Paul Tuttle, Designer*, exh. cat. (Santa Barbara: Santa Barbara Museum of Art, 1978).

Frederick A. Usher Jr.
1923–2009

A fixture in the Los Angeles design community, Frederick A. Usher Jr. specialized in exhibition design as well as graphic design at every scale, from magazines to environmental graphics. Usher's mastery of many disciplines reflected the broad education he received from Alvin Lustig, his mentor at Art Center School. The young Usher moved from his native Brooklyn to Los Angeles as a teen and worked briefly for Lustig. He then accepted a position with Charles and Ray Eames and honed his versatile skills on many projects, including the development of the wire chair. After leaving the Eames Office in 1953, Usher spent the rest of his career either working within architectural firms (both Victor Gruen and Frank Gehry were employers) or as principal of his own design practice. His long relationship with *Arts and Architecture* magazine included stints as both cover and layout designer and author (he was also the subject of articles), and he contributed to *Everyday Art*, a magazine for art educators published by the American Crayon Company. In 1960 he formed Usher-Follis, working with cofounder John Follis on such projects as the exhibition design of the Junior Science Laboratory at the Seattle World's Fair (1962) and graphics campaigns for several SeaWorld theme parks. After moving to Santa Barbara in 1970, Usher continued his design practice, notably creating signage and exhibits for the Monterey Bay Aquarium. In addition to his prolific design career, Usher was passionate about music, automobiles, and Latin culture. His deep roots in L.A.'s design community resulted in close friendships and collaborations with Carlos Diniz, Gere Kavanaugh, Marion Sampler, and Deborah Sussman, among others. BT

Sources
- Jack Brady and Tamara Kinsell, "Frederick Arthur Usher Jr., Designer," *Santa Barbara Independent*, June 18, 2009.
- Study files, Balch Art Research Library, LACMA, DEC.002.

Lydia Van Gelder
b. 1911

Fiber artist Lydia Van Gelder used a range of traditional weaving and fiber-dyeing techniques to create abstract woven compositions, often at architectural scale. She began experimenting with weaving while a student at the California School of Fine Arts in San Francisco in the 1930s. Early recognition soon followed for *Houses on a Street*, her handwoven wall hanging depicting an abstracted streetscape, which was made for the San Francisco Society of Women Artists' montage, a part of the Decorative Arts section curated by Dorothy Wright Liebes at the Golden Gate International Exposition (1939–40). After first settling in Lodi in 1936, she moved to Fresno in 1950 and then to Santa Rosa in 1963. In 1968 Van Gelder, who helped to form spinning and weaving guilds in Northern California, began a twenty-six-year tenure at Santa Rosa Junior College, where she taught spinning, dyeing, and weaving; the college's Frank P. Doyle Library organized a small retrospective of her work in 2008. During her long career she researched dyes, explored textile techniques, and earned an international reputation for her ikat work. She authored the books *Ikat: Techniques for Designing and Weaving* (1980) and *Ikat II: Ikat with Warp, Weft, Double, Compound Weaving, Shifu and Machine Knitting* (1996). The artist, who has exhibited nationally and internationally, was honored as a Living Treasure of Sonoma County in 1994. JMM

Sources
· Lydia Van Gelder study files, Cooper-Hewitt, National Design Museum, Smithsonian Institution.
· Patricia Lynn Henley, "Fabric of Her Life," April 2, 2008, www.bohemian.com/bohemian/04.02.08/visualarts-0814.html.

Van Keppel-Green
1939–early 1970s

As partners in the furniture and home accessories firm and retail establishment Van Keppel-Green, California-born designers Hendrik Van Keppel (1914–1988) and Taylor Green (1914–1999) created a highly successful line of affordable modern furnishings that epitomized the state's penchant for bright colors and indoor/outdoor living. Trained in art, Van Keppel first worked with architect Fritz Baldauf in San Francisco. He created his earliest designs out of enameled steel tubing and cotton cord upholstery in the 1930s and partnered with Green in 1939, initially designing for custom projects. Though Van Keppel-Green received some acclaim prior to World War II, the firm's popularity skyrocketed after 1945, when its designs began appearing in prominent exhibitions such as *Useful Objects* (MoMA, 1946) and the U.S. State Department's international traveling show *Design for Use, USA* (1951–53), and were sold in shops throughout the country. Van Keppel-Green used inexpensive materials—expanded metal, redwood, rattan, vibrantly colored enamel-coated steel tubing—to make products that appealed to cost-conscious middle-class consumers. The firm produced some lines in-house but contracted with local manufacturers such as Brown-Saltman and Brown Jordan on large production runs. Many of *Arts and Architecture* magazine's Case Study Houses were staged and furnished by the company, and Julius Shulman regularly used Van Keppel-Green's designs, especially its metal and cord chaise, in his photographs. The Van Keppel-Green showroom, established in 1948 in Beverly Hills, became a leading emporium of modern furnishings in Los Angeles, carrying the work of such California firms as Architectural Pottery and Heath Ceramics as well as prominent domestic and international brands. ss

Sources
- Marilyn Hoffman, "Confidence in Sound Modern Furniture Spurs California Design Team," *Christian Science Monitor*, March 17, 1954.
- "Simply Modern," *Designs*, August 1947, 8.
- "Tubular Steel, Cord, and Glass: Van Keppel-Green Combines Them in Furniture," *Interiors*, July 1947, 92–93.
- "Van Keppel-Green: California Team Which Designs and Makes Furniture," *House and Garden*, July 1947, 37.

Hendrik Van Keppel (left) and Taylor Green, 1954.

Vernon Kilns
1931–1958

Of the California potteries that capitalized on consumers' growing taste for bright colors in the 1930s, Vernon Kilns was the only "Big Five" manufacturer (see Gladding, McBean & Company) that had previously made dinnerware lines. The pottery's origins lie in the industrial city of Vernon, where Faye G. Bennison (1883–1974) bought Vernon China in 1931. Vernon Kilns first introduced solid-color dinnerware around 1934; the full *Early California* line was brought to market in 1935 in a range of glaze colors. Pastel glazes were added for the *Modern California* line in 1937. Utilizing the talents of designers Jane Bennison (Faye's daughter), Daniel Gale Turnbull, and sisters May Hamilton and Genevieve Hamilton, among others, the company executed innovative dinnerware and artware shapes with streamlined and moderne design elements. Other notable decorators included William "Harry" Bird, Donald Blanding, and artist Rockwell Kent, the latter designing the iconic *Salamina*, *Moby Dick*, and *Our America* patterns for the company. In addition to dinnerware, Vernon Kilns produced figurines, vases, and advertising and commemorative products. With the advent of World War II, demand for conventional floral dinnerware patterns grew, and Vernon responded by offering more traditional designs. A devastating fire destroyed the plant in 1946, but the factory was rebuilt and production resumed. Faye Bennison sold the Vernon Kilns trade name and equipment in 1958 to Metlox Manufacturing Company, which continued to produce Vernon dinnerware patterns for a short time thereafter. JMM

Sources
- Maxine Feek Nelson, *Collectible Vernon Kilns*, 2nd ed. (Paducah, Ky.: Collector Books, 2004).
- Study files, Balch Art Research Library, LACMA, DEC.002.

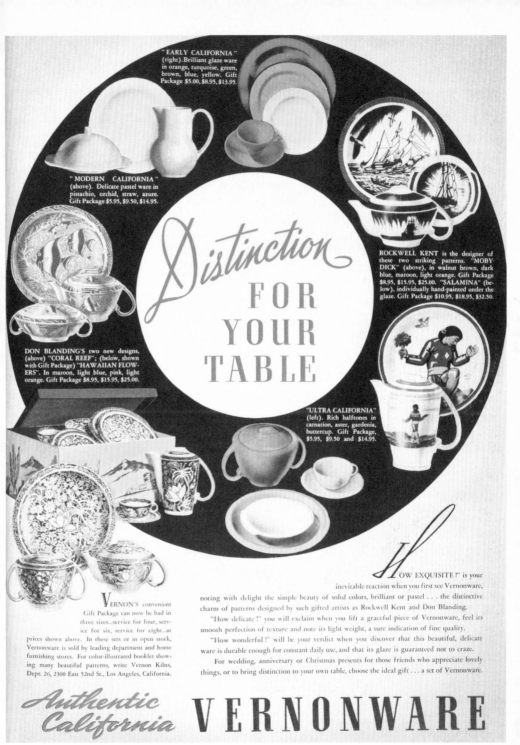

"EARLY CALIFORNIA" (right). Brilliant glaze ware in orange, turquoise, green, brown, blue, yellow. Gift Package $5.00, $8.95, $13.95.

"MODERN CALIFORNIA" (above). Delicate pastel ware in pistachio, orchid, straw, azure. Gift Package $5.95, $9.50, $14.95.

ROCKWELL KENT is the designer of these two striking patterns. "MOBY DICK" (above), in walnut brown, dark blue, maroon, light orange. Gift Package $8.95, $15.95, $25.00. "SALAMINA" (below), individually hand-painted under the glaze. Gift Package $10.95, $18.95, $32.50.

Distinction
**FOR
YOUR
TABLE**

DON BLANDING'S two new designs, (above) "CORAL REEF"; (below, shown with Gift Package) "HAWAIIAN FLOWERS". In maroon, light blue, pink, light orange. Gift Package $8.95, $15.95, $25.00.

"ULTRA CALIFORNIA" (left). Rich halftones in carnation, aster, gardenia, buttercup. Gift Package, $5.95, $9.50 and $14.95.

VERNON'S convenient Gift Package can now be had in three sizes...service for four, service for six, service for eight...at prices shown above. In these sets or in open stock, Vernonware is sold by leading department and home furnishing stores. For color-illustrated booklet showing many beautiful patterns, write Vernon Kilns, Dept. 26, 2300 East 52nd St., Los Angeles, California.

HOW EXQUISITE !" is your inevitable reaction when you first see Vernonware, noting with delight the simple beauty of solid colors, brilliant or pastel . . . the distinctive charm of patterns designed by such gifted artists as Rockwell Kent and Don Blanding.

"How delicate !" you will exclaim when you lift a graceful piece of Vernonware, feel its smooth perfection of texture and note its light weight, a sure indication of fine quality.

"How wonderful !" will be your verdict when you discover that this beautiful, delicate ware is durable enough for constant daily use, and that its glaze is guaranteed not to craze.

For wedding, anniversary or Christmas presents for those friends who appreciate lovely things, or to bring distinction to your own table, choose the ideal gift . . . a set of Vernonware.

Authentic California **VERNONWARE**

Vernon Kilns advertisement, 1939.

Vista Furniture Company

active 1950s–70s

Manufacturer of affordable modern furniture, Vista Furniture Company produced a range of practical forms—seating, storage units, desks, and bedroom sets—using inexpensive materials such as wood, plastic laminate, and iron in the form of tubes, rods, and expanded sheet (metal sheets that were perforated and pulled to create gridlike openings). Vista's signature look was the juxtaposition of brown wood and black iron, a combination popular in the post–World War II era. The company built a large factory on North Olive Street in Anaheim in 1953, having relocated its facilities from within the same city. Though they frequently commissioned California designers such as John Caldwell, Garry Carthew, Don Knorr, Stewart MacDougall, and Kipp Stewart, co-owners Don Bates and Jackson Gregory also created many of the designs themselves. The company's advertisements promised casual California furniture that was exceptionally priced, and its products were distributed in Los Angeles, San Francisco, New York, and Miami. Vista furniture appeared in the first six *California Design* exhibitions (1954–60) and was featured in *Arts and Architecture*, the *Los Angeles Times*, and *Living for Young Homemakers*. ss

Sources
· Study files, Balch Art Research Library, LACMA, DEC.002.

vista · casual californian

*smart designs
in 100 pieces

Vista Furniture Company advertisement, 1954.

Peter Voulkos
1924–2002

A pivotal yet contentious figure in the California craft community, Peter Voulkos broke from traditions of function, harmony, and balance in ceramics to explore the expressive possibilities of clay sculpture. He was the leader of an entire generation of craftspeople who rejected making functional objects and instead considered their work a means of personal expression or social commentary. Born Panagiotis Voulkos in Montana, the artist served in World War II and attended Montana State University in Bozeman (BS in Applied Art, 1951), where he took a required course in ceramics. Voulkos continued his studies at CCAC (MFA, 1952) and rapidly earned a national reputation for his well-executed stoneware. With fellow ceramist Rudy Autio, he helped build and served as resident manager of the Archie Bray Foundation for the Ceramic Arts in Helena, Montana, a ceramics school and community. In 1953, during the course of teaching a three-week summer session at North Carolina's Black Mountain College and spending time in New York City, Voulkos became aware of contemporary artistic developments, particularly the work of the Abstract Expressionists, and began to strive for a similar expressiveness and vigor in his work. He began to work clay in new ways—powerfully slinging the material, making violent slashes, and energetically applying slips and glazes to create sculptures that were often of monumental scale. The next year Millard Sheets, the newly appointed director of the Los Angeles County Art Institute, recruited Voulkos to head the school's ceramics program. Enlisting the help of area ceramists and his first student, Paul Soldner, Voulkos built the equipment for the department and fostered a feverish environment for radical experimentation in clay. He shared a studio with another student, John Mason, where a massive kiln could accommodate the large scale of the new work. In spring of 1959 Voulkos was terminated from the institute for his controversial activities but was hired immediately by the University of California, Berkeley, where he taught until his retirement in 1985. He shifted to making large-scale bronze sculptures after his move to Berkeley, although he returned to clay later in his career. In addition to numerous awards and solo museum exhibitions, Voulkos received a Guggenheim fellowship (1984) and a gold medal from the American Craft Council (1986). JMM

Sources
- Mary Davis MacNaughton, ed., *Clay's Tectonic Shift: John Mason, Ken Price, and Peter Voulkos 1956–1968*, exh. cat. (Claremont: Scripps College, 2012).
- Rose Slivka and Karen Tsujimoto, *The Art of Peter Voulkos*, exh. cat. (Tokyo: Kodansha International; Oakland: Oakland Museum, 1995).

The most prominent industrial designer working in California in the first half of the twentieth century, Kem Weber combined his modern European design education with personal interests in technology and efficiency and a commitment to making work suitable to its cultural and geographic context. Weber apprenticed with royal cabinet-maker Eduard Schultz and, after studying at the Kunstgewerbeschule (School of Fine and Applied Arts) in his native Berlin with reform architect Bruno Paul, joined the latter's office. He traveled to San Francisco in 1914 to oversee construction of the German section of the Panama-Pacific International Exposition; with the outbreak of World War I, he was stranded in the United States. In 1921 he moved to Los Angeles and became art director of the massive Barker Brothers furniture store, where in 1926 he created Modes and Manners, one of the first departments in the United States dedicated entirely to modern furniture and accessories, many of which were of his design. The following year he established his own firm in Hollywood. Weber's scope was broad—he designed furniture and products, as well as buildings and integrated interiors for hotels, shops, and private residences. The wide acclaim he received for the three-room apartment shown at Macy's Second International Exposition of Art in Industry (1928) significantly raised his national profile and resulted in commissions from manufacturers across the country, including furniture for Lloyd Manufacturing Company, Grand Rapids Chair Company, and Berkey and Gay Furniture Company, silver for Friedman Silver, and clocks for Lawson Time. His *Airline* chair, perhaps his best-known work, was designed to be assembled by the consumer from a kit of parts. The *Airline* was never widely available, but Walt Disney ordered several hundred for screening rooms at his new studio complex in Burbank in the late 1930s. As head of the industrial design department at Art Center School from the early 1930s until 1941, Weber taught a generation of designers who would shape the products and material life of the postwar period. After moving to Santa Barbara in 1945, he worked primarily as an architect, designing several private residences. BT

Sources
- Christopher Long, "Kem Weber and the Rise of Modern Design in Southern California," *The Magazine Antiques*, May 2009, 96–103.
- David Gebhard, "Kem Weber: Moderne Design in California, 1920–1940," *Journal of Decorative and Propaganda Arts*, Summer/Fall 1986, 20–31.
- David Gebhard and Harriette von Breton, *Kem Weber: The Moderne in Southern California, 1920–1941*, exh. cat. (Santa Barbara: The Art Galleries, 1969).

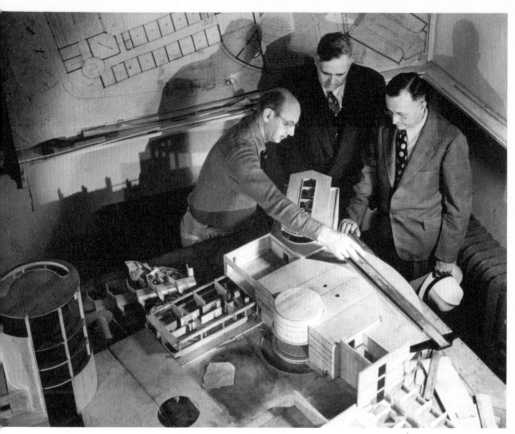

Kem Weber (left) discusses a proposed model of Art Center School, c. 1938.

A seminal figure in the Bay Area fiber art movement, artist and educator Katherine Westphal used collage, recycling, and photocopying techniques in her textile designs and works of art. A Los Angeles native, Westphal studied at Los Angeles City College before attending the University of California, Berkeley (BA, 1941; MA, 1943). She began her career teaching art at the University of Wyoming and the University of Washington. Following her marriage to Ed Rossbach, the couple moved to Berkeley in 1950, and Westphal studied printed textiles with Mary Dumas, a member of the decorative arts faculty at the university. From 1950 to 1958 she worked as a freelance textile designer, using screenprint, potato print, stencil, and other techniques to design patterns that she sold to manufacturers through an agent in New York. Using cut-up and reassembled remnants of her design samples, Westphal began creating art quilts in the early 1960s, one of which was exhibited in the Milan Triennale (1964). In 1966 the artist became a professor of design at the University of California, Davis, where she taught popular courses until 1979. In the late 1960s and early 1970s she began using the photocopier as a design tool and, with a Craftsman's Grant from the National Endowment for the Arts (1977–78), furthered her exploration of photographic and Xerox processes. Recipient of a gold medal from the American Craft Council (2009), she has worked in a wide range of media—jewelry, books, baskets, drawings, paintings, and ceramics—in addition to the art quilts and wearable art for which she is best known. JMM

Sources
- Katherine Westphal, interview by Carole Austin, September 3–6, 2002, Archives of American Art, Smithsonian Institution.
- Paul J. Smith, Jan Janeiro, and Susan Hay, *Ties That Bind: Fiber Art by Ed Rossbach and Katherine Westphal from the Daphne Farago Collection*, exh. cat. (Providence: Museum of Art, Rhode Island School of Design, 1997).
- Ed Rossbach and Katherine Westphal, interviews by Paul J. Smith, 1997, Archives of American Art, Smithsonian Institution.
- Katherine Westphal [Rossbach], "Artist and Professor," interview by Harriet Nathan, 1984, Regional Oral History Office, Bancroft Library, University of California, Berkeley, 1988.
- Jan Janeiro, "Piece Work: The World of Katherine Westphal," *American Craft* 48 (August/September 1988): 32–39.

Marguerite Wildenhain
1896–1985

A prolific potter and champion of the value of handcraft skills, Marguerite Wildenhain taught multitudes of students at her rural Pond Farm Pottery in the Russian River Valley. Born in France, Wildenhain studied at the Kunstgewerbeschule (School of Fine and Applied Arts) in Berlin and entered the Bauhaus ceramics course under professors Max Krehan and Gerhard Marcks in its first year (1919). In 1926 she became head of the ceramics department at the Municipal School of Fine and Applied Arts in Halle-Saale, Germany. During these years she designed dinnerware patterns for the royal German porcelain manufactory KPM, and in 1930 she married sculptor Frans Wildenhain. With the Nazis' rise to power in 1933, her position was terminated. The couple moved to Holland, where they established the studio pottery Het Kruikje ("Little Jug"). After the outbreak of World War II, Marguerite immigrated alone to California with the support of her distant cousins Jane and Gordon Herr. Together they established the Pond Farm Workshops in 1949, a school and community of craftspeople in Guerneville in Northern California. Both Trude Guermonprez and Victor Ries oversaw studios at Pond Farm in textiles and metalworking, respectively. Though the workshops were disbanded a few years later and Frans and Marguerite divorced, she continued to live, work, and run summer pottery courses at Pond Farm for the rest of her life. Her strident critiques of American art pedagogy were a prominent part of the postwar ceramics discourse, and she explained that "to be a craftsman apparently requires a definite attitude toward work and life, something evidently few schools are able to convey, something that cannot easily be taught in courses on techniques and theories."[1] As a teacher, she emphasized both the mechanics of potting and the discipline and dedication necessary for the pursuit of a craft. In her own work, Wildenhain primarily used high-fire stoneware, creating unique vessels decorated with abstract motifs or figural imagery, as well as ceramic figures inspired by her frequent trips to Central America and South America. She extended her influence through the publication of two books—*Pottery: Form and Expression* (1959) and the memoir *The Invisible Core: A Potter's Life and Thoughts* (1973). BT

1.
Marguerite Wildenhain, *Pottery: Form and Expression* (1959; repr., Palo Alto: Pacific Books, 1973), 11.

Sources
- Marguerite Wildenhain Papers, Archives of American Art, Smithsonian Institution.
- Dean and Geraldine Schwarz, eds., *Marguerite Wildenhain and the Bauhaus: An Eyewitness Anthology* (Decorah, Iowa: South Bear Press, 2007).
- Ruth R. Kath with Lawrence J. Thornton, *The Letters of Gerhard Marcks and Marguerite Wildenhain: A Mingling of Souls, 1970–1981* (Ames: Iowa State University Press, 1991).
- Lynn Colvin, ed., *Marguerite: A Retrospective Exhibition of the Work of Master Potter Marguerite Wildenhain*, exh. cat. (Ithaca, N.Y.: Cornell University, 1980).
- Marguerite Wildenhain, *The Invisible Core: A Potter's Life and Thoughts* (Palo Alto: Pacific Books, 1973).

Barbara Willis
1917–2011

As proprietor of a small Los Angeles pottery, Barbara Willis created mold-made ceramic wares imbued with a handmade look and feel. Born in Bakersfield, Willis moved with her family to Los Angeles, where she studied art and took ceramics courses with Laura Andreson at UCLA (BA, 1940). After she and fellow student Jean Rose established the short-lived Barbara-Jean Pottery Studio (1941–42), she founded Barbara Willis Pottery in early 1943 in a studio behind the garage of her family's home. Willis capitalized on the shortage of imported goods during World War II by producing an affordable line of practical forms such as vases, ashtrays, and figurines with details that suggested handcraft. The line was sold under the trade name Terrene Pottery in department stores nationwide. It was characterized by the juxtaposition of a textured bisque surface with brightly colored crackled glazes in white, yellow, aqua, and chartreuse. By 1945 Willis had purchased a North Hollywood property to accommodate her growing business, which employed about fifteen full-time staff at its peak. When Japanese imports began to undercut the California pottery market in the 1950s, Willis introduced new shapes and decaled designs in an attempt to broaden the appeal of her line, but ultimately she closed the pottery in 1958. Little was known about Willis until 1996, when she found one of her vases at a San Fernando Valley flea market and presented herself to the vendor. She then returned to working in clay, creating one-of-a-kind pieces. JMM

Sources
· Jack Chipman, *Barbara Willis: Classic California Modernism* (Venice, Calif.: Jaba Books, 2003).
· Mary Madison, "Ceramics from California Are Filling Gaps in Shops Here Because of Lack of Imports," *New York Times*, June 6, 1944.

Barbara Willis and husband Walter, c. 1946.

Jeweler and educator Byron Wilson used a language of geometric and organic forms to make modern jewelry out of largely inexpensive materials. Though he lacked formal training in metalwork, Wilson learned to manipulate metal from several jewelry repairmen in his native Oakland and learned to cast from a dental technician. A founding member of the Metal Arts Guild, he cited both the aesthetics and the philosophy behind the work of Margaret De Patta as important influences. Since his job as a claims inspector for the Southern Pacific Railroad left limited time for jewelry making, Wilson focused his efforts on work for exhibition and design competitions rather than for retail sale. A highlight of his exhibiting career was an honorable mention and purchase award for a necklace of silver, ebony, and ivory at the *Second Exhibition of American Jewelry and Related Objects* at the Memorial Art Gallery of the University of Rochester (1956). He preferred to use these semiprecious materials because of their pleasing color contrasts and relatively low cost. Wilson worked in both casting and hand raising and taught evening courses at CCAC for twenty-six years, where he trained many students and helped to build the school's first metal foundry. BT

Sources
- Toni Lesser Wolf, "Byron Wilson: The Gadget Man," *Metalsmith*, Winter 1992, 35–38.
- Study files, Balch Art Research Library, LACMA, DEC.002.

Bob Winston revived and championed the ancient process of lost-wax casting to make unique jewelry and sculptural pieces characterized by organic forms and contrasting textures. Born in Long Beach, Winston later moved to the Bay Area to study at the University of California, Berkeley (BA, 1940; MA, 1944). Beginning in 1942, he taught jewelry making and other art courses at CCAC, where he first began experimenting with the lost-wax casting method. By the mid-1940s Winston had earned a reputation as a respected craftsman and influential teacher. While he employed handwrought methods, he energetically promoted lost-wax casting for jewelry, emphasizing the sculptural and textural possibilities of the technique and insisting that although the medium was conducive to producing multiples, each of his creations was unique. He published *Cast Away*, a book on centrifugal and vacuum casting techniques, in 1970. Often referred to as San Francisco's most professional eccentric, Winston had a gregarious personality and was known for his unusual habits, such as carrying around his jewelry in a brown towel. In the late 1950s he resigned from CCAC to focus on jewelry making and later moved to Scottsdale, Arizona, where he established a studio and taught extension courses at several local universities. Winston returned to California in the late 1980s and settled in Concord. A founding member of the Metal Arts Guild, he exhibited in national shows of modern jewelry, including the influential *An Exhibition for Modern Living* (Detroit Institute of Arts, 1949), and in art festivals. In 1997 he was made a fellow of the American Craft Council. JMM

Sources
· Bob Winston, interview by Suzanne Baizerman, July 31–October 10, 2002, Archives of American Art, Smithsonian Institution.
· June Culp Zeitner, "Bob Winston, Modern Pioneer of Lost-Wax Casting," *Lapidary Journal*, July 1967, 558–63.
· Bob Winston, "Experiences with Lost-Wax Casting," in *Research in the Crafts* (New York: American Craftsmen's Council, 1961).

Born in San Francisco and raised in New York, Arnold Wolf worked as an industrial designer in Berkeley and made significant contributions to the field of audio design. After an early career as a child radio actor, Wolf took graphic design courses with art professor Harry Koblick at Los Angeles City College for two semesters before being drafted into World War II. Following the war, he studied dramatic art and historic decorative art at the University of California, Berkeley, graduating in 1952. A music aficionado, Wolf repaired stereo equipment in a Berkeley shop and soon began designing stereo components for the Oakland company Sargent-Rayment. These designs brought him to the attention of William Thomas, president of JBL—a leading L.A. audio equipment manufacturer—who asked Wolf to create loudspeaker enclosures for the company. Wolf's most spectacular and successful design was the 1957 *Paragon*, the first stereo speaker housed in a single cabinet that projected sound based on diffusion from a curved surface. A favorite of audiophiles for its high-quality sound, the *Paragon* remained in production until 1983. The walnut case incorporated elements of Scandinavian modern design, a popular style at the time. Wolf founded the firm Arnold Wolf Associates in 1957 and over his long career worked on many stereo enclosures for JBL as well as designs for consumer electronics, medical equipment, and cranes for handling containerized cargo. Wolf's talent was not limited to industrial design—in 1968 he redesigned JBL's logo and in 1969 became president of the company, serving for ten years. BT

Sources
· Lansing Heritage (website), www.audioheritage.org /html/people/wolf/wolf.htm.
· Study files, Balch Art Research Library, LACMA, DEC.002.

Potter and enamelist Jade Snow Wong made functional, elegant vessel forms known for their glowing color and subtle patterns. Born and raised in San Francisco's Chinatown, Wong studied economics and sociology at Mills College, discovering pottery only in her last semester in a class taught by F. Carlton Ball. She pursued her newfound interest in a summer course with Ball following her 1942 graduation and, while working at the Marin shipyard during World War II, began developing her skills as a member of the Mills College Ceramic Guild. It was at a guild meeting that she saw Ball demonstrate enameling. With the war over and a stock of pottery ready to sell, Wong established her studio in a Chinatown shop window. Her work sold quickly, and she soon set up a larger studio and began wholesaling to fine stores. By 1946 she had added enamels to her repertoire, and her work was included in major touring exhibitions in the late 1940s and 1950s. Her memoir, *Fifth Chinese Daughter* (1950), famously documents her life up to this point (a follow-up, *No Chinese Stranger*, was published in 1975). In 1950 she married Woodrow "Woody" Ong (1916–1985), who learned her craft and became her collaborator, spinning copper forms and managing the business, which moved to San Francisco's Jackson Square neighborhood in 1951. Wong wrote that her goal was to make "objects of beauty that could be used in the average home."[1] She ceased making pottery after Woody's passing but continued to work in enamel for the remainder of her life. JMM

1.
Maxine Hong Kingston, Kathleen Hanna,
Jade Snow Wong, and Forrest L. Merrill,
Jade Snow Wong: A Retrospective, 20.

Sources
· Maxine Hong Kingston, Kathleen Hanna, Jade Snow
Wong, and Forrest L. Merrill, *Jade Snow Wong:
A Retrospective*, exh. cat. (San Francisco: Chinese
Historical Society of America, 2002).

Owing to her flamboyant personality, Beatrice Wood was as renowned for her progressive attitude and avant-garde circle of friends as she was for her imaginative ceramics. Born to a prosperous San Francisco family, Wood was raised in New York and made frequent visits to Europe. In Paris she studied painting, drawing, and acting, but the advent of World War I forced her return to New York. Her involvement with the artistic avant-garde began when she met Marcel Duchamp in 1916. She worked with her lovers Duchamp and French writer Henri-Pierre Roché on the publication *The Blind Man*, exhibited with the Society of Independent Artists in 1917, and formed a friendship with modern art collectors Walter and Louise Arensberg. Wood moved to Los Angeles in 1928 to be close to the Arensbergs and Jiddu Krishnamurti, an Indian philosopher who had settled in Ojai and whose Theosophical beliefs she embraced. She took her first ceramics class at Hollywood High School in 1933 and by 1937 was selling pottery from a rented shop at the Crossroads of the World shopping court on Sunset Boulevard. Classes with Glen Lukens at USC followed, and later studies with Gertrud and Otto Natzler and with Otto and Vivika Heino advanced her knowledge of the medium. Her work attracted national attention, and she had her first solo show at America House in New York in 1944. In 1948 she moved to Ojai, where her mature glazing style emerged. Wood's voluminous output comprised many forms: vessels covered with iridescent luster glazes and applied decoration, figurative sculptures, and decorated plates, tiles, and plaques. She sold her home in Ojai to the Heinos and moved into her new home/studio/gallery nearby in 1974. Wood worked continuously throughout her long life, still making ceramics in the studio past her one hundredth birthday. JMM

Sources
· Beatrice Wood Papers, 1852–1998, Archives of American Art, Smithsonian Institution.
· *Beatrice Wood: Career Woman—Drawings, Paintings, Vessels, and Objects*, exh. cat. (Santa Monica: Santa Monica Museum of Art, 2011).
· Garth Clark, *Gilded Vessel: The Lustrous Art and Life of Beatrice Wood* (Madison, Wis.: Guild Publishing, 2001).
· Francis M. Naumann, ed., *Beatrice Wood: A Centennial Tribute*, exh. cat. (New York: American Craft Museum, 1997).

· Beatrice Wood, interview by Paul Karlstrom, March 2, 1992, and August 26, 1976, Archives of American Art, Smithsonian Institution.
· Beatrice Wood, *I Shock Myself: The Autobiography of Beatrice Wood* (San Francisco: Chronicle Books, 1985).

Ellamarie Woolley
1913–1976
Jackson Woolley
1910–1992

Known for their skillful exploitation of the vibrant colors and tactile appeal of enamel, Ellamarie and Jackson Woolley worked both collaboratively and as individuals in their exploration of the medium. Born and raised in San Diego, Ellamarie Packard studied art at San Diego State College and at Art Center School. She met Jackson Woolley at Francis W. Parker School, a high school in San Diego, where they both taught. A Shakespearean actor, Jackson was a Pittsburgh native who had studied theater at the Carnegie Institute of Technology and had moved to San Diego in 1935 to pursue his craft. The couple married in 1940, and Jackson completed a year of graduate study at the University of Washington before serving in the U.S. Army. Following World War II, Jackson studied art at Claremont Graduate School, though he did not complete his degree. After the Woolleys attended an enamel demonstration by Richard B. Petterson, they devoted themselves to learning enamel techniques and developing a production process that would allow them to create enough work to earn a living. They settled in San Diego, and from 1948 to 1953 created more than five thousand enameled plates and small vessels, each with bright colors and unique, Cubist-inspired designs. This work quickly attracted attention and was widely exhibited locally and nationally. By 1954 Ellamarie and Jackson were creating large-scale enamel panels, and between 1959 and 1965 they completed six enamel mural projects for institutions and businesses in California. In about 1970 Jackson ventured into other media, using synthetic materials such as fiberglass and polyester in his abstract constructions. With the assistance of a 1975 grant from the National Endowment for the Arts, Ellamarie created hard-edged geometric enamel designs that incorporated photo-screenprinting techniques. The Woolleys were honored with a two-artist show at the Museum of Contemporary Crafts in New York (1972), and Ellamarie's work was celebrated in a posthumous exhibition at the San Diego Fine Arts Gallery (1977). JMM

Sources
· Janice Keaffaber, "The Woolleys: Pioneers in Enamel," *Metalsmith* 13, no. 1 (Winter 1993): 28–37.
· *Ellamarie Woolley: A Retrospective Exhibition*, exh. cat. (San Diego: San Diego Fine Arts Gallery, 1977).
· Susan Peterson, "Ellamarie and Jackson Woolley," *Craft Horizons* 32, no. 3 (June 1972): 16–19.

Further Reading

Books, Articles, Exhibition Catalogues, and Films

- Adamson, Glenn, ed. *The Craft Reader*. Oxford: Berg, 2010.

- American Craftsmen's Council. *Asilomar*. Proceedings of the First Annual Conference of American Craftsmen, sponsored by the American Craftsmen's Council, June 12–14, 1957, Asilomar, California. New York: American Craftsmen's Council, 1957.

- ———. *Craftsmen of the Southwest*. New York: American Craftsmen's Council, [1965].

- ———. *Research in the Crafts*. Proceedings of the Fourth National Conference of the American Craftsmen's Council, August 26–29, 1961, Seattle, Washington. New York: American Craftsmen's Council, 1961.

- Armstrong, Elizabeth, ed. *Birth of the Cool: California Art, Design and Culture at Midcentury*, exh. cat. Newport Beach: Orange County Museum of Art; New York: Prestel Publishing, 2007.

- Bray, Hazel V. *The Potter's Art in California: 1855 to 1955*, exh. cat. Oakland: Oakland Museum, 1980.

- Byars, Mel. *The Design Encyclopedia*. 2nd ed. New York: Museum of Modern Art; London: Laurence King, 2004.

- Clark, Garth. *American Ceramics, 1876 to the Present*. New York: Abbeville, 1987.

- Cooke, Edward S., Jr., Gerald W. R. Ward, and Kelly H. L'Ecuyer. *The Maker's Hand: American Studio Furniture, 1940–1990*, exh. cat. Boston: Museum of Fine Arts, 2003.

- Creative Arts League of Sacramento and Crocker Art Museum. *The Creative Arts League Presents California Crafts XIV: Living Treasures of California*, exh. cat. Sacramento: Creative Arts League, 1985.

- Dailey, Victoria, Natalie Shivers, and Michael Dawson. *LA's Early Moderns: Art/Architecture/Photography*. Los Angeles: Balcony Press, 2003.

- Eidelberg, Martin, ed. *Design 1935–1965: What Modern Was: Selections from the Liliane and David M. Stewart Collection*, exh. cat. Montreal: Museum of Decorative Arts; New York: Abrams, 1991.

- Elliot-Bishop, James F., Christy Johnson, Elaine Levin, Jo Lauria, Harold B. Nelson, Billie P. Sessions, and Cécile Whiting. *Common Ground: Ceramics in Southern California, 1945–1975*, exh. cat. Pomona: American Museum of Ceramic Art, 2012.

- Emery, Olivia H. *Craftsman Lifestyle: The Gentle Revolution*. Pasadena: California Design Publications, 1977.

- Falino, Jeannine, ed. *Crafting Modernism: Midcentury American Art and Design*, exh. cat. New York: Museum of Arts and Design; New York: Abrams, 2011.

- Friedman, Mildred S. *Graphic Design in America: A Visual Language History*, exh. cat. Minneapolis: Walker Art Center, 1989.

- Greenbaum, Toni. "'California Dreamin': Modernist Jewelers in Los Angeles, 1940–1970." *Metalsmith* 22, no. 1 (Winter 2002): 38–47.

- ———. *Messengers of Modernism: American Studio Jewelry, 1940–1960*, exh. cat. Edited by Martin Eidelberg. Montreal: Museum of Decorative Arts; Paris: Flammarion, 1996.

- ———. "Tea and Jewelry: Modernist Metalsmithing in San Diego, 1940–1970." *Metalsmith* 22, no. 3 (Summer 2002): 26–33.

- Hall, Marian. *California Fashion: From the Old West to New Hollywood*. With Marjorie Carne and Sylvia Sheppard. New York: Abrams, 2002.

- Halper, Viki, and Diane Douglas. *Choosing Craft: The Artist's Viewpoint*. Chapel Hill: University of North Carolina Press, 2009.

- Hampton, Dave. *San Diego's Craft Revolution: From Post-War Modern to California Design*, exh. cat. San Diego: Mingei International Museum, 2011.

- Hiesinger, Kathryn B., and George Marcus. *Landmarks of Twentieth Century Design: An Illustrated Handbook*. New York: Abbeville, 1993.

- Hughes, Edan Milton. *Artists in California, 1786–1940*. San Francisco: Hughes Publishing, 1986.

- Jazzar, Bernard N., and Harold B. Nelson. *Painting with Fire: Masters of Enameling in America, 1930–1980*, exh. cat. Long Beach: Long Beach Museum of Art, 2006.

- Kaplan, Wendy, ed. *California Design, 1930–1965: Living in a Modern Way*, exh. cat. Los Angeles: Los Angeles County Museum of Art; Cambridge, Mass. MIT Press, 2011.

- Kennedy, Sarah. *The Swimsuit: A History of Twentieth-Century Fashions*. London: Carlton Books, 2010.

- Kent, Caroline Cochrane. *The Downey Museum of Art Presents: Southern California Industrial Pottery: 1927–1942*, exh. cat. Downey, Calif.: Downey Museum of Art, 1978.

- Koplos, Janet, and Bruce Metcalf. *Makers: A History of American Studio Craft*. Chapel Hill: University of North Carolina Press 2010.

- Lauria, Jo. *Color and Fire: Defining Moments in Studio Ceramics, 1950–2000: Selections from the Smits Collection and Related Works at the Los Angeles County Museum of Art*, exh. cat. Los Angeles: Los Angeles County Museum of Art; New York: Rizzoli, 2000.

Lauria, Jo, and Suzanne Baizerman. *California Design: The Legacy of West Coast Craft and Style.* San Francisco: Chronicle Books, 2005.

Lauria, Jo, Emily Zaiden, and Sharon K. Emanuelli. *Golden State of Craft: California 1960–1985*, exh. cat. Los Angeles: Craft in America, 2011.

L'Ecuyer, Kelly H. *Jewelry by Artists: In the Studio, 1940–2000.* Boston: Museum of Fine Arts, 2010.

Los Angeles County Museum of Art. *Salute to California: 50 Years of Fashion, 1930–1980*, exh. cat. Los Angeles: Los Angeles County Museum of Art, 1980.

Merrill, Todd, and Julie V. Iovine, eds. *Modern Americana: Studio Furniture from High Craft to High Glam.* New York: Rizzoli, 2008.

Nelson, Harold B., ed. *The House That Sam Built: Sam Maloof and Art in the Pomona Valley, 1945–1985*, exh. cat. San Marino, Calif.: Huntington Library, Art Collections, and Botanical Gardens, 2011.

Neuhart, Marilyn. *The Story of Eames Furniture.* With John Neuhart. Berlin: Gestalten, 2010.

Nordness, Lee. *Objects: USA*, exh. cat. New York: Viking, 1970.

Perry, Barbara, ed. *American Ceramics: The Collection of Everson Museum of Art.* New York: Rizzoli; Syracuse: Everson Museum of Art, 1989.

Reilly, Maureen. *California Casual Fashions, 1930s–1970s.* Atglen, Pa.: Schiffer, 2001.

Smith, Elizabeth A. T., et al. *Blueprints for Modern Living: History and Legacy of the Case Study Houses*, exh. cat. Los Angeles: Museum of Contemporary Art; Cambridge, Mass.: MIT Press, 1989.

Stern, Bill. *California Pottery: From Missions to Modernism*, exh. cat. San Francisco: Chronicle Books, 2001.

Stern, Jewel. *Modernism in American Silver: 20th-Century Design*, exh. cat. Edited by Kevin W. Tucker and Charles L. Venable. Dallas: Dallas Museum of Art; New Haven, Conn.: Yale University Press, 2005.

20 Outstanding L.A. Designers. DVD. Directed by Archie Boston, 1986. Los Angeles: Archie Boston Graphic Design, 2008.

Venable, Charles L., Ellen P. Denker, Katherine C. Grier, and Stephen G. Harrison. *China and Glass in America 1880–1980: From Tabletop to TV Tray*, exh. cat. Dallas: Dallas Museum of Art; New York: Abrams, 2000.

Wallance, Don. *Shaping America's Products.* New York: Reinhold, 1956.

Wood Turning Center and Yale University Art Gallery. *Wood Turning in North America Since 1930*, exh. cat. Philadelphia: Wood Turning Center; New Haven, Conn.: Yale University Art Gallery, 2001.

Periodicals

- *Architectural Forum.* New York: various publishers.
- *Arts and Architecture.* Los Angeles: John D. Entenza.
- *California Stylist.* Los Angeles: California Fashion Publications.
- *Communication Arts.* Palo Alto: Coyne & Blanchard.
- *Craft Horizons.* New York: American Craft Council.
- *Creative Crafts.* Los Angeles: Fred de Liden at Oxford Press.
- *Design Quarterly* (formerly *Everyday Art Quarterly*). Minneapolis: Walker Art Center.
- *Designs.* Hollywood, Calif.: Bottini Publishing House.
- *Everyday Art.* Sandusky, Ohio: American Crayon Company.
- *Everyday Art Quarterly* (later *Design Quarterly*). Minneapolis: Walker Art Center.
- *House and Garden.* New York: Condé Nast Publications.
- *House Beautiful.* New York: Hearst Corporation.
- *Interiors.* New York: Whitney Publications.
- *Los Angeles Times Home* magazine. Los Angeles: Los Angeles Times.
- *Print.* New Haven, Conn.: W. E. Rudge, Inc.

Archives and Libraries

- American Craft Council Library, Minneapolis.
- Archives of American Art, Smithsonian Institution, Washington, D.C.
- Architecture and Design Collection, Museum of Art, Design + Architecture, University of California, Santa Barbara.
- The Mr. and Mrs. Allan C. Balch Art Research Library, Los Angeles County Museum of Art, Los Angeles.
- Environmental Design Archives, University of California, Berkeley.
- The Getty Research Institute, Los Angeles.
- The Huntington Library, Art Collections, and Botanical Gardens, San Marino, California.
- Online Archive of California, www.oac.cdlib.org/.
- Paul Mills Library and Archive of California Art, Oakland Museum of California, Oakland.
- Regional Oral History Office, Bancroft Library, University of California, Berkeley.
- UCLA Center for Oral History Research, Charles E. Young Research Library, University of California, Los Angeles.

Acknowledgments

I am deeply grateful to the many individuals who participated in the production of this handbook. Contributing authors Jennifer Munro Miller, Lacy Simkowitz, and Staci Steinberger researched and wrote the majority of the entries. Their relentless pursuit of information and their thoughtful prose form the core of the book. Staci Steinberger also performed the remarkable feat of locating and acquiring nearly all of the portrait images that accompany each biography with efficiency and grace. These entries would have been very bare without the help of the designers and craftspeople, as well as their families and friends, all of whom generously provided information and answered many queries. Numerous librarians, archivists, curators, and scholars kindly shared their knowledge and resources. Project manager Nola Butler, LACMA's former head of publications, supported this project from its initial stages and shaped it in important ways. Irma Boom not only created a magnificent book design but also was a true collaborator in conceiving and developing some of the book's key elements. Wendy Kaplan has been a steadfast supporter and a sincere champion of this project, and I am especially appreciative of her extraordinary efforts to realize this book. In addition to her constant encouragement, her masterful editing of the manuscript resulted in clear and melodious text. Will Ferrell and Viveca Paulin-Ferrell and Peter and Shannon Loughrey recognized the importance of this volume at the outset, and their early contributions made it a reality. LACMA's Decorative Arts and Design Council; the Center for Craft, Creativity & Design; and the Elsie de Wolfe Foundation also made important, generous donations. Finally, my deepest thanks to all the individuals listed on the following page who contributed in various ways to the realization of this book. BT

Evelyn Ackerman
Jerome Ackerman
Cynthia Adler
Julia Armstrong-Totten
Jeremy Aynsley
Margaret Bach
Austen Barron Bailly
Wendy Hurlock Baker
Jennifer Bass
Jerry Berman
Anita Berry
Megan Berry
Meagan Blake
Irma Boom
Peter Brenner
Nola Butler
Chuck Byrne
Tripp Carpenter
Sasha Carrera
Edward Cella
Fiona Chen
Laura Cherry
Dane Cloutier
Elaine Lustig Cohen
James M. Conner
Luke Conover
Roger Conover
Lawrence Converso
Douglas Cordell
David Cressey
Donna Cressey
Victoria Dailey
Diana Daniels
Louis Danziger
Dale Brockman Davis
Judy Smith de Barros
Douglas Deeds
Rupert Deese
Robert Dirig
Jeanne Dreskin
Lynn Downey
Stephanie Dyas
Simon Elliott
Denny Lynn and George Engelke
Carol and Ian Espinoza
Arline Fisch
Russell Flinchum
Grant Follis
Heidi Fong
Miller Fong
Ted Fong
Melinda Gandara

Leigh Gleason
Michael Govan
Peggy Gruen
Susan Guadamuz
Eric Haeberli
Miranda Hambro
Dave Hampton
Jeffrey Hardwick
Barry Haun
Jeffrey Head
Maren Henderson
Robert J. Hennessey
Anthony Cromwell Hill
Tyrone Ironstone
Juliet Jacobson
Bernard Jazzar
Sam Jornlin
Lily Kane
John Kapel
Wendy Kaplan
Gere Kavanaugh
Henry C. Keck
Susan Landor Keegin
Tracy Kerr
Bernard Kester
Pat Kirkham
Karen Kitayama
Peter László
Jo Lauria
Damon Lawrence
Olga Lee
Malcolm Leland
Christopher Long
Michael Lordi
James Lovera
Waverly Lowell
Daniel Macchiarini
Jean Mathison
Catherine McIntosh
Harrison McIntosh
Marguerite McIntosh
Sue Medlicott
Lisa Melandri
Forrest L. Merrill
Jennifer Munro Miller
Noa Mohlabane
Julie Muñiz
Marlyn Musicant
Gail Reynolds Natzler
Harold Nelson
Maia November
Gerard O'Brien

Steve Oliver
Mark Ong
Daniel Ostroff
Harry Pack
Monica Paniry
Meg Partridge
Monica Penick
Jean Radakovich
merry renk
Mark Resnick
Florence Resnikoff
Victor Ries
Cheryle Robertson
Martin Roysher
Teresa Sanchez
Dale Schwamborn
June Schwarcz
Kay Sekimachi
Ben Serar
Piper Severance
Laura Ackerman Shaw
Sarah Sherman
Lacy Simkowitz
Evan Snyderman
Kaye Spilker
Jack Stauffacher
Staci Steinberger
Chris Stendahl
Bill Stern
Arlene Streich
Nina Stritzler-Levine
Deborah Sussman
Ondy Sweetman
Mattie Taormina
Gene Tepper
Adolph Tischler
Chris Travers
Frederick A. Usher Jr.
Xochitl Usher
Nerissa Dominguez Vales
Jennifer Watts
Katherine Westphal
Lorraine Wild
Hutton Wilkinson
Ana Wilson
Alexandra Griffith Winton
Arnold Wolf
Dianne Woo
Janice Woo
Claude Zachary
Aaron Ziolkowski
Jessica Zumberge

more

The Endless Sum

On any day of the year it's summer somewhere in the world
latest color film highlights the adventures of two young A
Robert August and Mike Hynson who follow this everla
round the world. Their unique expedition takes them to
Nigeria, South Africa, Australia, New Zealand, Tahiti, N
fornia. Share their experiences as they search the wor
fect wave which may be form-
ing just over the next Horizon. **BRUCE BROW**